W9

BEST
EUROPEA
FICTION
2010

EDITED
BY
ALEKSANDA
HEMON

FORTHCOMING IN JANU

This project is supported by cultural agencies throughout Europe and the US, and with primary support from Arts Council England.

WWW.DALKEYAR

GRANTA

12 Addison Avenue, London W11 4QR
email editorial@granta.com
To subscribe go to www.granta.com or call 845-267-3031 (toll-free 866-438-6150)

ISSUE 107

ACTING EDITOR	John Freeman
SENIOR EDITOR	Rosalind Porter
ONLINE EDITOR	Roy Robins
ASSOCIATE EDITORS	Helen Gordon, Liz Jobey
INTERNATIONAL EDITIONS EDITOR	Simon Willis
CONTRIBUTING WRITERS	Andrew Hussey, Robert Macfarlane, Xan Rice
DESIGN	Lindsay Nash, Carolyn Roberts
FINANCE	Geoffrey Gordon, Morgan Graver
MARKETING AND SUBSCRIPTIONS	Anne Gowan, Joanna Metcalfe
SALES DIRECTOR	Brigid Macleod
PUBLICITY	Pru Rowlandson
VICE PRESIDENT, US OPERATIONS	Greg Lane
TO ADVERTISE CONTACT	Emily Cook, ecook@granta.com
IT MANAGER	Mark Williams
PRODUCTION ASSOCIATE	Sarah Wasley
PROOFS	Lesley Levene
PUBLISHER	Sigrid Rausing
ASSOCIATE PUBLISHER	Eric Abraham

Granta USPS 000-508 is published five times per year (Feb, May, Jun, Aug & Nov) by *Granta* 12 Addison Avenue, London W11 4QR, United Kingdom at the annual subscription rate of $45.99
Airfreight and mailing in the USA by Agent named Air Business, C/O Worldnet Shipping USA Inc., 149-35 177th Street, Jamaica, New York, NY 11434. Periodicals postage paid at Jamaica NY 11431.
US POSTMASTER: Send address changes to *Granta*, PO Box 359 Congers, NY 10920-0359.

Granta is printed and bound in Italy by Legoprint. This magazine is printed on paper that fulfils the criteria for 'Paper for permanent document' according to ISO 9706 and the American Library Standard ANSI/NIZO Z39.48-1992.
This magazine has been printed on paper that has been certified by the Forest Stewardship Council (FSC).
Granta is indexed in the American Humanities Index.

Granta is grateful for permission to quote five lines from Leslie Fielder's Introduction to *Waiting for God* by Simone Weil. © GP Putnam's Sons, 1951.

A version of 'Body Snatchers' previously appeared in very abridged form in *Gear* magazine.

ISBN 978-1-929001-37-8

BOMB
OUTSPOKEN. INTIMATE. LEGENDARY.

CONVERSATIONS BETWEEN ARTISTS, WRITERS, ACTORS, DIRECTORS, MUSICIANS—SINCE 1981.

NUMBER 108 / SUMMER 2009 ON NEWSSTANDS JUNE 16
on the cover: Joe Bradley, *Schuperman*, 2009.

SUBSCRIBE
BOMBSITE.COM

"While New York publishers star-search for this year's single lollipop best-seller, Tin House recalls what literature can give one honest reader." —ALLEN GURGANUS

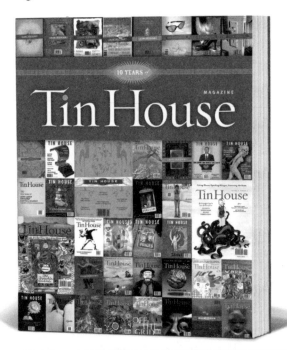

CONTENTS

Trick

The unexceptional mystery takes place:
around eleven, love turns to matter, Dad

dead. The ward grows and shrinks, early Spring
breaking promises through the glass.

Dad's untoothed mouth gawps, and its last
O holds one darkness; dark of a worked-out

abandoned mine. His absence is brute
absurdity, his hand soft as vellum.

His new state exposes the stark child of him,
and un-sons me. No answers now to a son's

questions, about this, about the sense,
for all his slightness, of a long life's mass

coming to rest, a settling that churns up
grief in a rounding cloud. Dad

dead; end of the opaque trick
that turns our gold to lead.

'Don't Touch Me'

S urrounded by beaten-up furniture, mismatched crockery and a wardrobe of second-hand cast-offs that would horrify Gok Wan, I am sometimes misperceived as an anti-materialist. To the contrary, I form passionate attachments to the lowliest of appurtenances, and the lowlier the better. Cleaning the porcelain, I take elaborate care not to shatter the chipped Victorian soap dish on the corner of the tub; last month, I squandered a full hour feverishly searching the kitchen for the elongated pewter teaspoon with which I have stirred my morning coffee for twenty years. The boot-sale soap dish and the 10p spoon are threaded through the warp of my daily life, and the longer anything is in my possession, the more it's not merely mine, it is me – as if we have exchanged molecules. Like most hoarders, I do not draw a clear divide between where the objective world stops and I begin.

If I am a fervent custodian of a bloody soap dish, imagine how this spiritual ventriloquism is raised to a power when the object at issue is something I made myself. Even a ratty potholder woven from old socks is not just what I have but what I am. Or so goes the pathetic fallacy. And I do mean pathetic. For this is the story of how my mistaking the *it* for the *I* led me to lose control to a degree that was unprecedented, even for a woman given as a girl to tantrums.

A New Yorker, at the age of thirty I moved to Belfast, where I lived for a dozen years. Early in that residence, I started working at the University of Ulster Art College on a series of ceramic figure sculptures. I wasn't enrolled for a degree; I'd a history of dabbling in the visual arts, and simply wanted to make stuff. Weekdays, I developed a routine: I would work on my latest novel until four p.m., then bike downtown to sculpt until the college closed at ten. They were long days, but fruitful ones.

I may have been contented pottering with mud while my cassette player blasted Kate Bush through the deserted studio, but the products of my labour betrayed that my personal life was a mess. The emotions the poses evoke range from dolefulness, pensiveness and exhaustion to full-tilt despond and despair, with an occasional break in the gloom for defiance. Short version: I had poor taste in men at the time, I was living by myself in a foreign country, and I was lonely. That sense of isolation and frustrated, free-floating desire permeated my figures with wistfulness, with sorrow, with yearning.

In many ways, the work is old-fashioned: representative and, if mildly abstracted, breaking no artistic ground. The forms are bony, sensual and sinuous. I am fond of elongation, attenuation, sometimes emaciation. Many of these figures are distinguished by oversized hands, their individual fingers frozen in mid-air (getting tiny rolls of wet clay to stay suspended was pretty fiddly). While the pieces were drying, students continually banged past them and broke the hands, so I'd have to wet the clay back down and painstakingly form the fingers all over again. Even once fired, those long ceramic fingers were still tyrannically fragile. As the faculty informed me, I was working 'on the edge of the material', and in hindsight I probably shouldn't have been fashioning these forms in clay to begin with.

Among the twenty-some surviving pieces is a seated figure titled 'Don't Touch Me'. When I sculpted it, I was going out with a chap in many ways a lovely man – which made him an unusual choice, alas – but one who also suffered from a dodgy psychiatric history. Sudden flashes of paranoia and hostile emotional withdrawal marred many an erstwhile pleasant evening, and to call the relationship volatile would be an understatement. Nevertheless, I felt very tenderly towards F.

Thus, in this deliberately androgynous sculpture, I tried to capture some of his sensitivity, benevolence and, in the Buddha-like position, a certain repose – for between obsessive outbursts of unwarranted jealousy and suspicion, F could be perceptive, intuitive and self-possessed. Yet the head is averted, flinching. The counterpoint to the figure's tranquillity especially resides in the hands – their fingers pulled back in recoil, fending off approach. (Delightfully, a friend once observed that the figure looks as if he's typing, the averted head reading from a page.) The emotional content of this sculpture is vested in those hands, in the delicacy of each suspended finger, whether it is recoiling from love, or merely poised to strike the caps-lock key.

The fact that I can still talk about these objects in the present tense is nothing short of miraculous. Transport and storage of the ridiculously breakable sculptures have been a massive pain in the backside. Just getting them from the art college three miles home to my house in Belfast required a commercial roll of bubble wrap so enormous that I could not embrace its circumference. The pieces can't be stacked, so when I moved to London they didn't fit in the van. I stashed them in my landlords' attic, made a second trip to Belfast to schlep them into a friend's garage when my landlords sold their house, drove with my partner in a rented van from London to retrieve them – only to miss the Stranraer ferry by five minutes and drive back down the length of England empty-handed – then made a *second* trip in *another* rental van, at which point we did make the ferry, and hauled them all the way back to our flat in Borough. Which is where they remain today. 'Don't Touch Me', for example, sits on a storage cabinet beside the toilet. The rest are bundled under the bed or shoved atop wardrobes.

One of the leading reasons I've never shifted out of my overpriced rental is that I do not want to move my sculptures again. For that matter, these frail neurotic wards may help to explain why, after twenty-two years, I still live in Britain. However fiercely they might be crated, I cannot imagine shipping these stupid things across the Atlantic; they'd never make it in one piece. Yet I'm too selfishly attached to them, too convinced they are not simply by me but *are* me, to give them to friends. Manacled to ceramic, I am stuck here, pitifully illustrating the paradigm of the owned owning the owner.

Fast forward to a few years ago, when my boiler was on the fritz. As luck would have it – bad luck – for the first time my regular plumber, P, showed up at the door with his twelve-year-old son in tow. The quiet, biddable boy struck me as terribly sweet, as a tradesman taking his kid to work also struck me as sweet. I left them to it. Since the boiler was in the kitchen, I'd no reason to expect him to be tinkering in the loo.

Unfortunately, I now know that the main connection to this flat's water supply is right behind the storage cabinet beside the toilet.

'I, uh—' P nervously interrupted me in my study. 'I have to show you something, and it's kind of bad.'

I followed him to the loo. 'Don't Touch Me' was sitting on the floor. It did not belong on the floor, ever, where it would be easily kicked, and I never, either, let anyone else move my sculptures. For good reason, too, since I didn't need P's fluttering little hand gesture to absorb the fact that three amputated fingers now littered the lino.

Okay, one cry of dismay would have been understandable. All the bother of lugging that sculpture from drying shelf to kiln to house to garage to London flat, only for it to be bashed by a thoughtless plumber. But an initial shriek was just the beginning. I kept shrieking. Oh, I can remember a few things I must have said, but the content paled before the delivery. I screamed at him so harshly and at such length that I went hoarse.

It's frustrating that exaggeration is such a routine literary device, making many an incident sound embellished for effect when to the contrary it is impossible to express just how really, really awful a scene it became. In clinical terms, the fit I threw that morning must have qualified as proper 'hysteria', a word we often employ with loose, hyperbolic carelessness. Such an absolute loss of self-control was actually frightening. Verbal abuse alternated with temple-clutched mooing, or screams so strained that they made almost no sound. The glaring futility of this eruption – the fact that no invective I hurled at this poor plumber would make my sculpture whole again – only drove me to greater frenzy.

For minutes paralysed with horror, finally the plumber pushed past me and threw his tools in his kit. 'I've never been talked to like that in all my life,' he said (and I don't doubt it). Sweeping out the front door, he announced on the landing that he was 'never coming back to this flat again' (as indeed he hasn't done), and then he called for his son.

As the boy skittered downstairs with his father, I felt physically sick. I'd forgotten about the son.

That expression 'blind rage' has something to it, since I had failed even to see the boy at the periphery of my narrowed, spotty vision. It was bad enough that my *grand mal* seizure had immediately transposed who was the culprit and who the victim here. But the boy! The boy changed everything. To have given that plumber such a dressing down *in front of his son* was criminal. Worse still, if it could get worse, as I shuffled back into the flat I realized that the boy, not his father, might credibly have been the author of that breakage, in which case I had just vented the full force of my harridan's wrath on a twelve-year-old.

While nothing mended is ever quite the same again, I did repair those fingers, grinding charcoal into epoxy resin to produce a matt-black glue and holding them in place one at a time with the mounted cross-lock tweezers from my metalsmithing days. Yet the disreputable display with which 'Don't Touch Me' is now associated has marred the piece far more than any plumber ever did. A long letter of profuse, grovelling apology did not elicit a reply, and it didn't deserve one.

Having so disgraced myself, I've been forced to examine what, exactly, this attachment is really to. Memory, perhaps – of Belfast, of F, of the long, deliciously wordless nights of smoothing a plane here, adjusting a limb there, dancing a private jig to Talking Heads. But I have the memories without their totems. Certainly I am inordinately attached to any external manifestation of – forgive the schlocky language, but what other word suffices? – my soul. Thus writing is my ideal medium. Visual artists who produce one-of-a-kind pieces must choose between retaining their handiwork and abdicating it to others. Ease of duplication allows writers the eating and having of cake: to both keep their work and give it away.

Yet the deepest attachment is to my own capacity to make stuff. I've not sculpted for many years. The longer I've forgone an activity that once gave me such pleasure, the more precious these figures have grown as emblems of a part of myself that is receding from reach. (I have a recurrent and rather heavy-handed dream in which I wander a big house and come upon a dusty, disused room full of art supplies.) Were I ever to return to sculpture, I wouldn't need my old work, or at least I wouldn't take a plumber's head off when he or his young son knocked into one. I'd know I could make new sculptures, which would probably come out better. Chances are that I'd happily chuck some of the less successful earlier efforts in the bin.

In lieu of that liberation, I am weighed down by little hands that tug at my shirtsleeves. I will never leave this flat. I am drowning in bubble wrap. ∎

LOST CAT

Mary Gaitskill

Almost two years ago I lost my cat Gattino. He was very young, still a kitten, at seven months barely an adolescent. He is probably dead but I don't know for certain. For two weeks after he disappeared people claimed to have seen him; I trusted two of the claims because Gattino was blind in one eye, and both people told me that when they'd caught him in their headlights, only one eye shone back. One guy, who said he saw my cat trying to scavenge from a garbage can, said that he'd looked 'really thin, like the runt of the litter'. The pathetic words struck my heart. But I heard something besides the words, something in the coarse, vibrant tone of the man's voice that immediately made another emotional picture of the cat: back arched, face afraid but excited, brimming and ready before he jumped and ran, tail defiant, tensile and crooked. Afraid but ready; startled by a large male, that's how he would've been. Even if he was weak with hunger. He had guts, this cat.

Gattino disappeared two and a half months after we moved. Our new house is on the outskirts of a college campus near a wildlife

LOST CAT NEEDS HELP

GATTINO IS A 7-MONTH OLD, SLENDER GRAY
MALE TABBY WITH DISTINCTIVE SPOTS AND
STRIPES. HE'S BLIND IN HIS RIGHT EYE. IF YOU
FIND HIM, PLEASE CONTACT MARY AT 845-758-
4598 or PETER AT 845-758-2703. HE MAY LOOK
LIKE A STRAY BECAUSE HE IS THIN, HAS A BAD
EYE AND A CHRONIC RESPIRATORY INFECTION.
BUT HE HAS A HOME AND WE ARE HEART-SICK
TO HAVE LOST HIM

preserve. There are wooded areas in all directions, and many homes with decrepit outbuildings sit heavily, darkly low behind trees, in thick foliage. I spent hours at a time wandering around calling Gattino. I put food out. I put a trap out. I put hundreds of flyers up. I walked around knocking on doors, asking people if I could look in their shed or under their porch. I contacted all the vets in the area. Every few days, someone would call and say they had seen a cat in a parking lot or behind their dorm. I would go and sometimes glimpse a grizzled adult melting away into the woods, or behind a building, or under a parked car.

After two weeks there were no more sightings. I caught three feral cats in my trap and let them go. It began to snow. Still searching, I would sometimes see little cat tracks in the snow; near dumpsters full of garbage, I also saw prints made by bobcats or coyotes. When the temperature went below freezing, there was icy rain. After a month I stopped looking. Nearly every day I sat and looked out the window at the field across from our house, tears running down my face.

Six months after Gattino disappeared my husband and I were sitting in a restaurant having dinner with some people he had recently met, including an intellectual writer we both admired. The writer had considered buying the house we were living in and he wanted to know how we liked it. I said it was nice but it had been partly spoiled for me by the loss of our cat. I told him the story and he said, 'Oh, that was your trauma, was it?'

I said yes. Yes, it was a trauma.

You could say he was unkind. You could say I was silly. You could say he was priggish. You could say I was weak.

A few weeks earlier, I had had an email exchange with my sister Martha on the subject of trauma, or rather tragedy. Our other sister, Jane, had just decided not to euthanize her dying cat because she thought her little girls could not bear it; she didn't think she could bear it. Jane lives in chronic pain so great that sometimes she cannot move normally. She is under great financial stress and is often responsible for the care of her mother-in-law as well as the orphaned children of her sister-in-law who died of cancer. But it was her cat's approaching death that made her cry so that her children were frightened. 'This is awful,' said Martha. 'It is not helping that cat to keep him alive, it's just prolonging his suffering. It's selfish.'

Martha is in a lot of pain too, most of it related to diabetes and fibromyalgia. Her feet hurt so badly she can't walk longer than five minutes. She just lost her job and is applying for disability which, because it's become almost impossible to get, she may not get, and which, if she does get, will not be enough to live on, and we will have to help her. We already have to help her because her health insurance – and she has the discount kind – payments are so high that her unemployment isn't enough to cover them. This is painful for her too; she doesn't want to be the one everybody has to help. And so she tries to help us.

She has had cats for years, and so considers herself something of an expert; she wanted to help Jane by giving her advice, and she sent me several emails wondering about the best way to do it. Finally she forwarded me the message she had sent to Jane, in which she urged her to put the cat down. When she didn't hear from Jane, she emailed me some more, agonizing over whether or not Jane was angry at her, and wondering what decision she would make regarding the cat. She said, 'I'm afraid this is going to turn into an avoidable tragedy.'

Impatient by then, I told her that she should trust Jane to make the right decision. I said, this is sad, not tragic. Tragedy is thousands of people dying slowly of war and disease, injury and malnutrition. It's Hurricane Katrina, it's the war in Iraq, it's the earthquake in China. It's not one creature dying of old age.

After I sent the email, I looked up the word 'tragic'. According to *Webster's College Dictionary*, I was wrong; their second definition of the word is 'extremely mournful, melancholy or pathetic'. I emailed Martha and admitted I'd been wrong, at least technically. I added that I still thought she was being hysterical. She didn't answer me. Maybe she was right not to.

★

I found Gattino in Italy. I was in Tuscany visiting Beatrice von Rezzori, who, in honour of her deceased husband, the writer Gregor von Rezzori, has made her estate, Santa Maddalena, into a small retreat for writers. Beatrice knew that I love cats and she told me that down the road from her two old women were feeding a yard full of semi-wild cats, including a litter of kittens who were very sick and going blind. Maybe, she said, I could help them out. No, I said, I wasn't in Italy to do that, and anyway, having done it before, I know it isn't an easy thing to trap and tame a feral kitten. 'Oh,' she said, 'I thought you liked cats.'

The next week one of her assistants, who was driving me into the village, asked if I wanted to see some kittens. Sure, I said, not making the connection. We stopped by an old farmhouse. A gnarled woman sitting in a wheelchair covered with towels and a thin blanket greeted the assistant without looking at me. Scrawny cats with long legs and narrow ferret hips stalked or lay about in the buggy, overgrown yard. Two kittens, their eyes gummed up with yellow fluid and flies swarming around their asses were obviously sick but still lively – when I bent to touch them, they ran away. But a third kitten, smaller and bonier than the other two, tottered up to me mewing weakly, his eyes almost glued shut. He was a tabby, soft grey with strong black stripes. He had a long jaw and a big nose shaped like an eraser you'd stick on the end of a pencil. His big-nosed head was goblin-ish on his emaciated pot-bellied body, his long legs almost grotesque. His asshole seemed disproportionately big on his starved rear. Dazedly he let me stroke his bony back – tentatively, he lifted his pitiful tail. I asked the assistant if she would help me take the kittens to a veterinarian and she agreed; this had no doubt been the idea all along.

The healthier kittens scampered away as we approached and hid in a collapsing barn; we were only able to collect the tabby. When we put him in the carrier, he forced open his eyes with a mighty effort, took a good look at us, hissed, tried to arch his back and fell over. But he let the vets handle him. When they tipped him forward and lifted his tail to check his sex, he had a delicate, nearly human look of puzzled dignity in his one half-good eye, while his blunt muzzle expressed stoic

large, beautiful marble that had belonged to my father; sometimes I took it out of my pocket and held it up in the sun as if it might function as a conduit for his soul.

My father died a slow painful death of cancer, refusing treatment of any kind for as long as he was able to make himself understood, gasping 'no doctors, no doctors'. My mother had left him years before; my sisters and I tended to him, but inadequately, and too late – he had been sick for months, unable to eat for weeks at least before we became aware of his condition. During those weeks I thought of calling him; if I had I would've known immediately that he was dying. But I didn't call. He was difficult, and none of us called him often. Once, when I held the marble up in the sun, I wondered if a little bit of my father's soul had been reincarnated in the body of this kitten so that I would have a chance to love him better. I didn't really believe this. But it did occur to me. My father had been an orphan too.

My husband did not like the name Chance and I wasn't sure I did either; he suggested McFate, and so I tried it out. McFate grew stronger, grew a certain one-eyed rakishness, an engaged forward quality to his ears and an eagerness in the attitude of his neck that was gallant in his fragile body. He put on weight, and his long legs and tail became soigné, not grotesque. He had strong necklace markings on his throat; when he rolled on his back for me to pet him, his belly was beige and spotted like an ocelot. In a confident mood, he was like a little gangster in a zoot suit. Pensive, he was still delicate; his heart seemed closer to the surface than normal, and when I held him against me, it beat very fast and light. McFate was too big and heartless a name for such a small fleet-hearted creature. '*Mio Gattino*,' I whispered, in a language I don't speak to a creature who didn't understand words. '*Mio dolce piccolo gatto*.'

One night when he was lying on his back in my lap, purring, I saw something flash across the floor; it was a small, sky-blue marble rolling out from under the dresser and across the floor. It stopped in the middle of the floor. It was beautiful, bright, and something not visible to me had set it in motion. It seemed a magical and forgiving omen, like the presence of this loving little cat. I put it on the windowsill next to my father's marble.

. I spoke to my husband on the phone about taking Gattino home with us. I said I had fallen in love with the cat, and that I was afraid that by exposing him to human love I had awakened in him a love that was unnatural and perhaps too big for him. I was afraid that if I left him he would suffer a loneliness that he never would have known had I not appeared in his yard. My husband said, 'Oh no, Mary...' but in a bemused tone.

I would understand if he'd said it in a harsher tone. Many people would consider my feelings neurotic, a projection on to an animal of my own loneliness and fear. Many people would consider it almost offensive for me to lavish such love on an animal when I have by some standards failed to love my fellow beings: for example, orphaned children who suffer every day, not one of whom I have adopted. But I have loved people; I have loved children. And it seems that what happened between me and the children I chose to love was a version of what I was afraid would happen to the kitten. Human love is grossly flawed, and even when it isn't, people routinely misunderstand it, reject it, use it or manipulate it. It is hard to protect a person you love from pain because people often choose pain; *I* am a person who often chooses pain. An animal will never choose pain; an animal can receive love far more easily than even a very young human. And so I thought it should be possible to shelter a kitten with love.

I made arrangements with the vet to get me a cat passport; Gattino endured the injection of an identifying microchip into his slim shoulder. Beatrice said she could not keep him in her house, and so I made arrangements for the vet to board him for the two weeks Peter and I travelled.

Peter arrived; Gattino looked at him and hid under the dresser. Peter crouched down and talked to him softly. Then he and I lay on the bed and held each other. In a flash, Gattino grasped the situation: the male had come. He was friendly. We could all be together now. He came on to the bed, sat on Peter's chest and purred thunderously. He stayed on Peter's chest all night.

We took him to the veterinarian the next day. Their kennel was not the quiet, cat-only quarters one finds at upscale American animal hospitals. It was a common area that smelled of disinfectant and fear. The vet put Gattino in a cage near that of a huge enraged dog who barked and growled, lunging against the door of its kennel. Gattino looked at me and began to cry. I cried too. The dog raged. There was a little bed in Gattino's cage and he hid behind it, then defiantly lifted his head to face the gigantic growling; that is when I first saw that terrified but ready expression, that willingness to meet whatever was coming, regardless of its size or its mercilessness.

When we left the vet I was crying so hard that Beatrice's assistant, a man named Carlo, stopped to get me some water at a roadside fountain. In Italian, he said to my husband, 'When I die I want to be reborn as Mary's cat. I have never seen anyone love anything so much.' But I was not crying exclusively about the kitten, any more than my sister Jane was crying exclusively about euthanizing her old cat. At the time I didn't realize it, but I was, among other things, crying about the children I once thought of as mine.

Caesar and his sister Natalia are now twelve and sixteen respectively. When we met them in 2002, they were six and ten. We met him first. We met him through the Fresh Air Fund, an organization that brings poor urban children (nearly all of whom are black or Hispanic) up by bus to stay with country families (nearly all of whom are white). The Fresh Air Fund is an organization with an aura of uplift and hope about it, but its project is a difficult one that frankly reeks of pain. In addition to Caesar, we also hosted another little boy, a seven-year-old named Ezekiel. Imagine that you are six or seven years old and that you are taken to a huge city bus terminal, herded on to buses with dozens of other kids, all of you with big name tags hung around your neck, driven for three hours to a completely foreign place, and presented to total strangers with whom you are going to live for two weeks. Add that these total strangers, even if they are not rich, have materially more than you could ever dream of, that they are much bigger than you and, since you are staying in their house, you are supposed to obey them. Add that they are white as sheets. Realize that even very young black children have often learned that white people are essentially the enemy. Wonder: who in God's name thought this was a good idea?

And here is one more element to consider: we wanted to love these children. I fantasized about serving them meals, reading to them at night, tucking them in. Peter fantasized about sports on the lawn, riding bikes together. We were aware of the race-class thing. But we thought we could override it. You could say we were idealistic. You could say we were selfish and stupid. I don't know what we were.

We were actually only supposed to have one, and that one was Ezekiel. We got Caesar because the FAF called from the bus as it was on its way up full of kids and told us that his host family had pulled out at the last minute due to a death in the family, so could we take him? We said yes because we were worried about how we were going to entertain a single child with no available playmates; I made the FAF representative promise that if it didn't work out, she would find a backup plan. Of course it didn't work out. Of course there was no backup plan. The kids hated each other, or, more precisely, Ezekiel hated Caesar. Caesar was younger and more vulnerable in every way: less confident, less verbal, possessed of no athletic skills. Ezekiel was lithe, with muscular limbs and an ungiving facial symmetry that sometimes made his naturally expressive face cold and mask-like. Caesar was big and plump, with deep eyes and soft features that were so generous they seemed nearly smudged at the edges. Ezekiel was a clever bully, merciless in his teasing, and Caesar could only respond by ineptly blustering, 'Ima fuck you up!'

'Look,' I said, 'you guys don't have to like each other, but you have to get along. Deep down, don't you want to get along?'

'No!' they screamed.

'He's ugly!' added Ezekiel.
'Dry up Ezekiel,' I said. 'We're all ugly, okay?'
'Yeah,' said Caesar, liking this idea very much. 'We're all ugly!'
'No,' said Ezekiel, his voice dripping with malice, 'you're ugly.'
'Try again,' I said. 'Can you get along?'
'Okay,' said Caesar. 'I'll get along with you Ezekiel.' And you could hear his gentle, generous nature in his voice. You could hear it, actually, even when he said, 'Ima fuck you up!' Gentleness sometimes expresses itself with the violence of pain or fear and so looks like aggression. Sometimes cruelty has a very charming smile.
'No,' said Ezekiel, smiling. 'I hate you.'
Caesar dropped his eyes.

I don't mean to suggest that while I was in Italy I was heartbroken about the children. I didn't yet realize how much I had to be heartbroken about. I sent them postcards; I bought them little gifts. We were in Florence for a week. It was beautiful, but crowded and hot, and I was too full of sadness and confusion to enjoy myself. Nearly every day I pestered the vet, calling to see how Gattino was. 'He's fine,' they said. 'The dog isn't there any more. Your cat is playing.' I wasn't assuaged. I had nightmares; I had a nightmare that I had put my kitten into a burning oven, and then watched him hopelessly try to protect himself by curling into a ball; I screamed in pain to see it, but could not undo my action.

Peter preferred Ezekiel and Caesar knew it. I much preferred Caesar, but we had made our original commitment to Ezekiel and to his mother, whom we had spoken with on the phone. So I called the FAF representative and asked her if she could find another host family for Caesar. 'Oh great,' she snapped. But she did come up with a place. It sounded good: a single woman, a former schoolteacher, experienced host of a boy she described as responsible and kind, not a bully. 'But don't tell him he's going anywhere else,' she said. 'I'll just pick him up and tell him he's going to a pizza party. You can bring his stuff over later.'

'Okay,' I said, and then promptly took him out to a park to tell him. I said, 'You don't like Ezekiel, do you?' and he said, 'No, I hate him.' I asked if he would like to go stay at a house with another boy who would be nice to him, where they would have a pool and— 'No,' he said. 'I want to stay with you and Peter.' I couldn't believe it – I did not realize how attached he had become. But he was adamant. We had the conversation three times, and none of those times did I tell him he had no choice. I pushed him on the swing set and he cried, 'Mary! Mary! Mary!' And then I took him home and betrayed him.

Peter told Ezekiel to go into the other room and we sat Caesar down and told him he was leaving. 'No,' he said. 'Send the other boy away.'

Ezekiel came into the room.

'Send him away!' cried Caesar.

'Ha ha,' said Ezekiel, 'you go away!'

The FAF woman arrived. I told her what was happening. She said, 'Why don't you just let me handle this.' And she did. She said, 'Okay, Caesar, it's like this. You were supposed to go stay with another family but then somebody in that family *died* and you couldn't go there.'

'Somebody *died*?' asked Caesar.

'Yes, and Peter and Mary were *kind* enough to let you come stay with them for a little while and now it's time to—'

'I want to stay here!' Caesar screamed and clung to the mattress.

'Caesar,' said the FAF woman. 'I talked to your mother. *She* wants you to go.'

Caesar lifted his face and looked at her for a searching moment. 'Lady,' he said calmly, 'you a liar.' And she was. I'm sure of it. Caesar's mother was almost impossible to get on the phone and she spoke no English.

This is probably why the FAF woman screamed, actually screamed, 'How dare you call me a liar! Don't you ever call an adult a liar!'

Caesar sobbed and crawled across the bed and clutched at the corner of the mattress; I crawled after him and tried to hold him. He cried, 'You a liar too Mary!' and I fell back in shame.

The FAF lady made a noble and transparently insincere offer.

'Caesar,' she said, 'if you want, you can come stay with me and my family. We have a big farm and dogs and—'

He screamed, 'I would never stay with you lady! You're gross! Your whole family is gross!'

I smiled with pure admiration for the child.

The woman cried, 'Oh I'm gross, am I!' And he was taken down the stairs screaming, 'They always send me away!'

Ezekiel darted around, actually blocking the exit at one point as if he did not want Caesar to be carried out, his body saying, please don't do this, but his mouth spitefully whispering, 'Ha ha! You go away! Ha ha!'

I walked outside and watched Peter carrying the sobbing little boy into the woman's giant SUV. Behind me Ezekiel was dancing on the other side of the screen door, incoherently taunting me as he sobbed too, breathless with rage and remorse.

If gentleness can be brutish, cruelty can sometimes be so closely wound in with sensitivity and gentleness that the cruel one winds up deforming and humiliating his own soul. Animals are not capable of this. That is why it is so much easier to love an animal. Ezekiel loved animals; he was never cruel with them. Every time he entered the house, he greeted each of our cats with a special touch. Even the shy one, Tina, liked him and let him touch her. Caesar, on the other hand, was rough and disrespectful – and yet he wanted the cats to like him. One of the things he and Ezekiel fought about was which of them Peter's cat Bitey liked more.

On the third day in Florence I called Martha – the sister I later scolded for being hysterical about a cat – and asked for help. I asked her to communicate psychically with Gattino. She said she would. She said I needed to do it too. 'He needs reassurance,' she said. 'You need to tell him every day that you're coming back.'

I know how foolish this sounds. I know how foolish it is. But I needed to reach for something with a loving touch. I needed to reach even if nothing was physically there within my grasp. I needed to reach even if I touched darkness and sorrow. And so I did it. I asked Peter to do it too. We would go to churches and kneel on pews and pray for Gattino. We were not alone; the pews were always full of people, old, young, rich and poor, of every nationality, all of them reaching, even if nothing was physically there. 'Please comfort him, please help him,' I asked. 'He's just a little thing.' Because that was what touched me: not the big idea of tragedy, but the smallness and tenderness of this bright, lively creature. From Santa Annunziata, Santa Croce and Santa Maria Novella, we sent messages to and for our cat.

I went into the house to try and comfort Ezekiel, who was sobbing that his mother didn't love him. I said that wasn't true, that she did love him, that I could hear it in her voice – and I meant it, I had heard it. But he said, 'No, no, she hates me. That's why she sent me here.' I told him he was lovable and in a helpless way I meant that too. Ezekiel was a little boy in an impossible situation he had no desire to be in, and who could only make it bearable by manipulating and trying to hurt anyone around him. He was also a little boy used to rough treatment, and my attempts at caring only made me a sucker in his eyes. As soon as I said 'loveable' he stopped crying on a dime and starting trying to get things out of me, most of which I mistakenly gave him.

Caesar was used to rough treatment too – but he was still looking for good treatment. When I went to visit him at his new host house, I expected him to be angry at me. He was in the pool when I came and as soon as he saw me, he began splashing towards me, shouting my name. I had bought him a life jacket so he would be more safe in the pool and he was thrilled by it; kind treatment did not make me a sucker in his eyes. He had too strong a heart for that.

But he got kicked out of the new host's home anyway. Apparently he called her a bitch and threatened to cut her. I could see why she wouldn't like that. I could also see why Caesar would have to let his anger out on somebody if he didn't let it out on me.

Ezekiel was with me when I got the call about Caesar's being sent home. The FAF woman who told me said that Caesar asked her if he was going back to his 'real home, with Peter and Mary'. I must've looked pretty sick when I hung the phone up because Ezekiel asked, 'What's wrong?' I told him, 'Caesar got sent home and I feel really sad.' He said, 'Oh.' There was a moment of feeling between us – which meant that he had to throw a violent tantrum an hour later, in order to destroy that moment.

After Ezekiel left I wrote a letter to Caesar's mother. I told her that her son was a good boy, that it wasn't his fault that he'd gotten sent home. I had someone translate it into Spanish for me, and then I copied it on to a card and sent it with some pictures I had taken of Caesar swimming. It came back: MOVED, ADDRESS UNKNOWN. Peter told me that I should take the hint and stop trying to have any further contact. Other people thought so too. They thought I was acting out of guilt and I was. But I was acting out of something else too. I missed the little boy. I missed his deep eyes, his clumsiness, his generosity, his tenderness. I called the Fresh Air Fund. The first person I talked to wouldn't give me any information. The next person gave me an address in East New York; she gave me a phone number too. I sent the letter again. I prayed the same way I later did for Gattino: 'Spare him. Comfort him. Have mercy on this little person.' And Caesar heard me – he did. When I called his house nearly two months after he'd been sent back home, he didn't seem surprised at all.

Gattino heard us too. In the past, when I have left other cats with a sitter for two weeks, on my return the animal acts like it doesn't know me any more; I have to coax it back. But when Peter and I returned to the veterinary hospital to claim Gattino he purred at the sight of us. When we went back to Santa Maddalena, his little body tensed with wonder when he saw the room we had lived in together; he walked through it as if returning to a lost kingdom. My body relaxed too; I felt safe. I felt as if I had come through a kind of danger, or at least a kind of complex maze, and that I had discovered how to make sense of it. Beatrice was gracious and welcoming; the estate seemed a layered dream of natural beauty and human endeavour.

Peter was swimming in the pool – I had just emerged from it – when Beatrice put down the phone and said, 'Bad news.' A mutual friend, a writer I have known since the Eighties, had just lost his young wife of less than a year. They had been swimming in the Gulf of Mexico when a wave picked her up and smashed her on a coral reef. We talked about it for maybe twenty minutes. I went to email him a message of support. Then we continued to lay about the pool. The heat was thick and delicious, the trees and foliage variously textured and gently moving. There were bottles of fizzy water and little cups for espresso placed near our seats. Insects hummed and lilted. The beauty was like a film, a gauze floating over the red coral reef, the man holding the dying woman in his arms, the pain of her broken body entering his. The ocean surging around them, teaming with brilliant life.

The next day we went home. The trip was a two-hour ride to Florence, a flight to Milan, a layover, an eight-hour Atlantic flight, then another two-hour drive. At Florence Peter was told that because of an impossible bureaucratic problem with his ticket, he had to leave the terminal in Florence, get his bag and recheck it for the flight to Milan. The layover wasn't long enough for him to recheck the bags and make it on to the flight with me, and the airline (Alitalia) haughtily informed him that there was no room on the next flight. I boarded the plane alone; Peter had to spend the night in Milan and buy a ticket on another airline; I didn't find this out until I landed in New York with Gattino peering intrepidly from his carrier.

And Gattino *was* intrepid. He didn't cry in the car, or on the plane, even though he'd had nearly nothing to eat since the night before. He settled in patiently, his slender forepaws stretched out regally before him, watching me with a calm, confidently upraised head. He either napped in his carrier or sat in my lap, playing with me, with the person sitting next to me, with the little girl sitting across from me. If I'd let him, he would've wandered the aisles with his tail up. This is very unusual for a cat on an airplane. Like I said, he had guts. More than me. More than most people.

★

The first time I called Caesar, he asked about Bitey; he asked about his life jacket. We talked about those things for a while. Then I told him that I was sad when he left. He said, 'Did you cry?' And I said, 'Yes. I cried.' He was silent; I could feel his presence so intensely, like you feel a person next to you in the dark. I asked to talk to his mother – I had someone with me who could speak to her in Spanish – to ask her for permission to have contact with her son. I also spoke to his sister Natalia. Even before I met her, I could hear her big, fleshy beauty in her voice – curious, vibrant, expansive in its warmth and longing.

I sent them presents – books mostly, and toys when Caesar's birthday came. I talked more to Natalia than to her brother; he was too young to talk to for long on the phone. She reached out to me with her voice as if with her hand, and I held it. We talked about her trouble at school, her fears of the new neighbourhood, her mother's boyfriend in prison, movies she liked, which were mostly about girls becoming princesses. When Caesar talked to me, it was half-coherent stuff about cartoons and fantasies. But he could be suddenly very mature. 'I want to tell you something,' he said once. 'But I don't know what it is.'

I wanted to meet their mother; I very much wanted to see Caesar and meet his sister. Peter was reluctant, but he was willing to do it for me. We went to East New York with a Spanish-speaking friend. We brought board games and cookies. Their mother kissed us on both cheeks and gave us candles. She said they could come to visit for Holy Week – Easter. Natalia said, 'I'm so excited'; I said, 'I am too.'

And I was. I was so excited I was nearly afraid. When Peter and I went into Manhattan to meet them at Penn Station, it seemed a miracle to see them there. As soon as we got to our house Caesar threw a tantrum on the stairs – the scene of his humiliation. But this time I could keep him, calm him and comfort him. I could make it okay, better than okay. Most of the visit was lovely. It is hard to remember now how lovely it was. But the pictures in our photo album say that it was: pictures of them riding their bikes down the street on a beautiful spring day; of them painting Easter eggs. We took Natalia to a riding stable; we have a picture of her getting ready to mount a horse with an expression of mortal challenge on her face; we have another of her sitting atop the horse in a posture of utter triumph.

On the way back to New York on the train, Caesar asked, 'Do you like me?' I said, 'Caesar, I not only like you, I love you.' He looked at me levelly and said, 'Why?' I thought a long moment. 'I don't know why yet,' I said. 'Sometimes you don't know why you love people, you just do. One day I'll know why and then I'll tell you.'

When we introduced Gattino to the other cats we expected drama and hissing. There wasn't much. He was tactful. He was gentle with the timid cats, Zuni and Tina, slowly approaching to touch noses, or following at a respectful distance, sometimes sitting near Tina and gazing at her calmly. Bitey had passed away and we had gotten a new cat, a tough young female named Biscuit. He teased and bedevilled Biscuit – and it's true that she didn't love him. But she accepted him.

I thought, here is something good.

Then things began to go wrong – little things at first. I discovered I'd lost my passport; Peter lost a necklace I'd given him; I lost the blue marble from Santa Maddalena. For the sixth summer in a row, Caesar came to visit us and it went badly. My sister Martha was told she was going to be laid off. We moved to a new house located on Bard College Campus; everything went wrong: the landlord had left old junk all over the building; the stove was broken and filled with nests of mice; one of the toilets was falling through the floor; windowpanes were broken.

But the cats loved it. Especially Gattino. The yard was spectacularly beautiful and wild, and when he turned six months old, we began letting him out for twenty minutes at a time, always with one of us in the yard with him. We wanted to make sure he was cautious and he was; he was afraid of cars, he showed no desire to go into the street, or really even out of the yard, which was large. We let him go out longer. Everything was fine. The house got cleaned up; we got a new stove. Somebody actually found Peter's necklace and gave it back. Then one day I had to go out for a couple of hours. Peter wasn't home. Gattino was in the yard with the other cats; I thought, *He'll be okay.* When I came back he was gone.

Because he had never gone near the road I didn't think he would cross the street – and I thought if he had, he would be able to see his way back, since across the street was a level, low-cut field. So I looked behind our house, where there was a dorm in a wooded area, and to both sides of us. Because we had just moved in, I didn't know the terrain and so it was hard to look in the dark – I could only see a jumble of foliage and buildings, houses, a nursery school and what I later realized was a deserted barn. I started to be afraid. Maybe that is why I thought I heard him speak to me, in the form of a very simple thought that entered my head, plaintively, as if from outside. It said, 'I'm scared.'

I wish I had thought back, 'Don't worry. Stay where you are. I will find you.' Instead I thought, 'I'm scared too. I don't know where you are.' It is crazy to think that the course of events might've been changed if different sentences had appeared in my mind. But I think it anyway. Gattino was attuned to me. I think he could feel me even from far away; I think feeling fear from me further unmoored him. But I could not help it; fear overtook me.

The next day I had to go into Manhattan because a friend was doing a public reading from her first new book in years. Peter looked for Gattino. Like me he did not look across the street; he simply didn't think he would've gone there.

The second day we made posters and began putting them up in all the dorms, houses and campus buildings. We alerted campus security, who put out a mass email to everyone who had anything to do with the college.

The third night, just before I went to sleep, I thought I heard him again. 'I'm lonely,' he said.

The fifth night we got the call from a security guard saying that he saw a small, thin, one-eyed cat trying to forage in a garbage can outside a dorm. The call came at two in the morning and we didn't hear it because the phone was turned down. The dorm was very close by; it was located across the street from us, on the other side of the field.

I walked across the field the next day and realized something about it that I had not noticed before: from a human perspective it was flat enough to look across easily; from the perspective of a creature much lower to the ground, it was made of valleys and hills too big to see over.

Something I didn't say correctly: I did not lose the blue marble from Santa Maddalena. I threw it away. When Peter lost his necklace I decided that the marble was actually bad luck. I took it out into a field and threw it away.

A friend offered to pay for me to see a psychic. He hadn't seen her, he doesn't see psychics. But a pretty girl he was flirting with had seen this psychic and been very impressed by her; my friend wanted me to tell him what the psychic was like, I guess in order to know if the girl was a crank or not. So I made the appointment. She told me that Gattino was 'in trouble'. She told me he was dying. She couldn't tell me where he was, except that it was down in a gulley or ditch, someplace where the ground dropped suddenly; water was nearby and there was something on the ground that crunched underfoot. Maybe I could find him. But maybe I wasn't meant to. She thought maybe it was his 'karmic path' to 'walk into the woods and close his eyes', and, if that was so, that I shouldn't interfere. On the other hand, she said, I might still find him if I looked in the places she described.

I told my friend that I was not impressed with the pretty girl's choice of psychics. And then I went to the places she described and looked for Gattino. I went every day and every night. At the end of one of those nights, when I was about to go to sleep, words appeared in my head again. They were, 'I'm dying.'

I thought, *He is an animal. He can face death better than you.* I thought, *Respect him.* More words came: 'I love you.' And then 'Goodbye.'

I got up and took a sleeping pill. Two hours later I woke with tears running down my face.

★

Who decides which deaths are tragic and which are not? Who decides what is big and what is little? Is it a matter of numbers or physical mass or intelligence? If you are a little creature or a little person dying alone and in pain, you may not remember or know that you are little. If you are in enough pain you may not remember who or what you are; you may know only your suffering, which is immense. Who decides? What decides? Common sense? Can common sense dictate such things? Common sense is an excellent guide to social structures – but does it ever have anything to do with what moves you?

After that first Easter visit, Caesar and Natalia came up for two weeks during the summer. We went biking and swimming and to the movies and the Dutchess County Fair. Natalia started the first of her horseback riding lessons; in subsequent visits she would work at the stable for free just to be near the horses she loved. In the evenings she and I had a ritual of 'walking at night', during which we would walk around the neighbourhood and talk intimately. She told me that she had lied to me when she'd said earlier that she was doing well in school; she admitted that she was failing. I asked her if she wanted to do better. She said yes. I asked if she would like me to help her with her homework on the phone at night, and she said, 'Yes.'

Peter was primarily 'in charge' of Caesar – but they did not have a bond. Peter didn't like the boy's combination of neediness and aggression. The kid would hang on Peter and always want his attention and if he didn't get it, which he often did not, he would say something like, 'When I get older I'm going to knock your teeth out.' He said it like a joke, and he was after all a small child. But physically he wasn't small; neither he nor his sister was small in that sense, and one took what they said seriously because of it. I took Caesar's aggression seriously – but for a long time I forgave it. I forgave because for me the aggression and need translated almost on contact as longing for the pure affection he had been denied by circumstance and outrage at the denial. His father had after all left him; his mother – who was in her mid-forties – worked long hours at a factory and so left the children alone often. When she got home she was usually too tired to do more than cook dinner; Caesar said she cursed him regularly. Both children believed she preferred her four grown kids living in the Dominican Republic to them.

But nonetheless she loved them, especially Caesar. You could see it in their bodies when they were together, see it in the way she looked at him when she greeted him as 'my beautiful son'. She loved both children, and she beat them. She beat them rationally as punishment, and irrationally, seemingly just as a way of relating. Once when I was on the phone with Natalia, helping her write an essay, she said, 'Just a minute, I need to get another pencil.' She put the phone down, said something to her mother in a light, questioning voice – and was answered with violent shouts that turned into crashes and scuffling and Natalia sobbing before the phone was slammed into its cradle. The mother sometimes attacked the children as if she was a child herself, pulling Natalia's hair or scratching her. She demeaned Natalia, continually. Caesar she infantilized, bathing him and brushing his teeth for him even when he was nine years old; if Peter hadn't insisted that he tie his own shoes he might never have learned how – his mother ordered Natalia to do it, and so did he.

We had met a couple of school social workers when we came to serve as chaperones on a school trip: they told us they already knew about the beatings, or thought they did; Natalia would report being beaten, and then take it back, saying she'd been lying. If she had bruises, she refused to show them. The kids had once been put into foster care, and Natalia never wanted that to happen again. One of the social workers believed the kids were being abused and thought they should be taken away from their mother; the other thought Natalia was a manipulative liar and felt sorry for the mother, whom she had known for years. 'She loves those kids,' said the woman. 'She works her ass off for them.'

And they loved her, passionately; their self-esteem was completely bound up with her. At the end of one Christmas visit, when I took the children back to Penn Station, their mother didn't show up to meet me. The children were scared and hurt; I took them to an apartment we shared with a friend and comforted them, singing and combing Natalia's hair, and reassuring them that their mother would soon call my cell and let us know what had happened. After a couple of hours, I thought we should call the police. Caesar immediately stopped crying and looked at me with eyes on fire. 'Mary,' he said, 'if you do that I will hate you for ever.' They didn't want the police involved. They were afraid they would be taken away from their mother.

And so we bit our tongues and tried not to speak critically to the children of their mother. We found a person who could speak Spanish to translate for us, and we tried to consult her about the kids whenever possible (her advice was usually something like, 'Just punch him in the mouth'), to show respect for her in front of them, to work with the situation.

We had the kids up for Christmas, Easter, sometimes on their birthdays, and always for at least a few days in the summer. We occasionally met them in the city too. I worked with Natalia on the phone, helping her read assigned books and write reports on them. I also hired a tutor for her, paying a college student to go out to Brooklyn once a month to give her math lessons. Her teacher said she was improving. Then other kids began to jeer at her for it. They spat on her in the lunchroom and she got into fights. But she didn't talk about that. She would call me and cry and say she couldn't do well in school because of her mother beating her. I said, 'You don't have control over your mother. You have control over yourself.' I said, 'Please; keep trying.' She was quiet for a moment. She said, very calmly, 'Mary, I don't think I can.' I said, 'Just try.' But I could hear that she could not. I could hear it in her voice. I can't put into words why she could not. But I could hear it.

She kept doing her homework on the phone with me. She kept meeting the math tutor. But even though she did the assignments, she didn't turn them in. She would say she had, that the teacher was lying, that the teacher had torn them up, that the teacher hated her. The teacher said she never saw the work.

I kept looking for Gattino. I didn't think in particular about the children while I looked for him. I barely thought at all. I tried to feel the earth, the sky, the trees and wet, frozen stubble of ground. But I couldn't feel anything but sad. Once when I was driving to a shelter to check if he had been turned in, I heard a story on the radio about Blackwater contractors shooting into a crowd of Iraqi civilians. They killed a young man, a medical student, who had gotten out of his car. When his mother leaped from the car to hold his body, they killed her. I hear stories like this every day and I realize they are terrible stories. But I don't feel anything about them. When I heard this one, I felt it like my heart had been torn open.

It was the loss of the cat that had made this happen; his very smallness and lack of objective consequence had made the tearing open possible. I don't know why this should be true. But I am sure it is true.

True not just of my heart; my mind also tore. I called another psychic, a pet psychic, and asked her about Gattino. She told me he had died, probably of kidney failure after drinking something toxic. She said he had suffered. I called another one. She said he had died, but that he hadn't suffered, that he had 'curled up as if he were going to sleep'. I began asking random people if they had any 'psychic feeling' about the cat; I am still amazed at how many claimed that they did. Some of them were friends, some were acquaintances, some were complete strangers. A stranger, an innkeeper in Austin, told me that he was sicker than I realized and that he had gone away to die in order to spare me any suffering; she said that he loved me. Then she put her arms around me and made purring sounds – and I made them back! An acquaintance, a taciturn and generally unfriendly woman who works in a stable, and whom I would not have thought to ask for psychic input, looked at the poster I showed her and her partner, and remarked in a low voice, just as I was about to walk away, 'For whatever it's worth, I don't think your cat's dead.' She thought he was living in or under a white house with a lot of walkways around it. It sounded like a description of half the dorms on campus.

And so, in the middle of January I put another round of posters up on campus and in mailboxes. I started getting calls almost immediately from people saying that they had seen a small one-eyed cat. I started leaving food in the places he was supposed to have been, to keep him there. I also left scraps of my clothes near the food, so he might catch my scent and remember me. I left food in our backyard. I collected turds and piss clumps from the litter boxes and scattered them in our yard so that he might catch the scent of our other cats and be guided home by it. I collected a whole shopping bag of turds and piss and then went out late one night to make a trail of it from the far edge of the field to our house. The snow was up to my calves and it took me almost an hour to get through it, diligently strewing used litter in the path of my footsteps.

I asked Peter if he thought I was crazy. He said that sometimes he did think that. But then he thought of friends of his whose twin daughters had recently died of a rare skin disease called recessive dystrophic epidermylosis. When the girls were born, their parents were told they should put them in an institution. When they insisted on taking them home, the doctors just shrugged and gave them some bandages. Nothing was known about home care; the parents had to learn it all themselves. They devoted themselves to the care of their children, and they gave them nearly normal lives; in spite of excruciating pain involved in almost every ordinary activity, including eating, the girls played sports, went to college, flirted online and had boyfriends with whom they had sex. They hoped for a cure until they died at twenty-seven. Their parents worked right up until the end to make their lives as good or at least as unpainful as possible. 'We would've done anything,' said their mother. 'If someone had told us it would help to smear ourselves with shit and roll in the yard we would've done it.'

'But they didn't actually do it,' I said.

'Well,' said Peter, 'no one told them to.'

Because Natalia said she was afraid to go to the public junior high school, we paid for she and her brother to go to Catholic school. Caesar did okay; she got kicked out in a couple of months. Her mother laughed bitterly. She said, 'Natalia will always cause trouble.' I said, 'I still believe in her.' There was incredulous silence on the other end of the phone.

A friend of mine said to me, 'You can't go against the mother. Don't even try. The child will always follow her lead. You can't compete.'

'I know,' I said. 'I won't try.'

I did know. And I tried. I told myself I wasn't trying, but I was.

That summer, we sent them to a camp that was supposed to be great for screwed-up kids, and it was great, especially for Natalia. She excelled, the counsellors loved her and invited her to participate in their year-long Teen Leadership programme, which provided group phone calls with counsellors and other kids, tutoring in school and weekend trips up to the camp every month. Natalia was thrilled, and when we returned her to her mother we showed her the pictures of Natalia at camp, getting along with everybody and not causing trouble. Her mother looked at the pictures and literally dropped them on the ground.

Natalia made the first two trips to camp and then stopped showing up. She stopped participating in the group phone calls. She stayed out all night and skipped school. She said it was because her mother beat her. Her mother said it was because she wanted to have sex and do drugs.

When she came up to visit for Christmas we had a fight; afterwards I tried to talk to her. She said, 'I don't care. I don't care about nothing.' I said I doubted that was true. She said, 'It is true. It's always been true.' And I felt her relief in saying it. 'All right,' I said. 'It might be true sometimes, but not all the time. Almost everybody cares about something, some time.' She looked at me sullenly; she did not disagree. 'But,' I said, 'if you walk around acting like you don't care for long enough, people will start to believe you. If you really don't care, then people who do care will leave your life and people who don't care will come in to it. And if that happens, you will find yourself in a very terrible place.' As I spoke her face slowly opened; slowly, her sullenness revealed fear. I kissed her and said, 'It doesn't have to be that way.' A few months later she ran away from home.

Caesar was nine when his sister ran away, and I could sense him watching her with very wide eyes. He joined his mother in condemning her, but even when he did, I could still hear affection for her in his voice. He loved his family – but he loved me too. I could talk to him about anything, about dreams, heaven and hell, what made a person evil and why a picture was good or bad. When he noticed the picture of my father in the glassed-in cabinet that functions as a sort of shrine, he wanted to know about him. I told him that my father was orphaned by the death of his mother when he was nine, followed by the death of his father a year later. Then his dog died. Still, when the World War broke out, my father wanted to enlist. He joined the war at Anzio, one of the most terrible battles. Caesar said, 'I feel bad for your father. But I don't feel sorry for him. Because he sounds like a terrific person.' Later, when Peter asked if Caesar had ever had an imaginary friend, he said, 'I didn't before but I do now. My imaginary friend is Mary's father.'

When my father was dying I asked him something. I did not really ask him; I don't think he was conscious and I whispered the question rather than spoke it. But nonetheless it was a serious question. 'Daddy,' I said, 'tell me what you suffered. Tell me what it was like for you.' I could never have asked him in life. But I believed that on the verge of death he could 'hear' my whispered words. And slowly, over a period of time, I believe I have been answered, at least in part. I felt that I was hearing part of the answer while I was out looking for my cat, when it was so cold and so late no one else was around. It occurred to me then that the loss of the cat was in fact a merciful way for me to have my question answered.

Both my sisters and I sat with my father when he was dying; we all took care of him with the help of a hospice worker who stopped by every day. But Martha was alone with him when he died. She said that she had felt death come into the room. She said that death felt very gentle. Later she told us that she felt and even saw terrible things before he died. But she seemed at peace about witnessing his death.

When she returned home she had few people to talk to about what had happened. Martha was not close to the people she worked with and they were not ideal confidants. But she had few others. When she described my father's life to a co-worker, he found it absurd that Martha seemed to place as much emphasis on the death of my father's dog as she did on the death of his parents, and he spoke to her coolly. 'I love dogs,' he said. 'I'm sad when a dog dies. But no dog should ever be compared to family.' I don't remember what Martha said in response; I dimly remember that she seemed to have struggled with what to say, that her voice sounded thin and frustrated when she described it to me.

When I was out looking for the cat, so late that no one else was around, I remembered this story, and I wished I had been with my sister when her co-worker spoke to her that way. I would have said, 'Imagine you are a nine-year-old boy and you have lost your mother. You are in shock and because you are in shock you are reduced to a little animal who knows its survival is in danger. So you say to yourself, "Okay, I don't have a mom. I can deal with that." And then the next year your father dies. You think, "a'ight. I don't have a dad either. I can deal with that too." Then your dog dies. And you think, "Not even a dog? I can't even have a dog?" I would've said, "Of course the dog didn't mean as much to him as his parents did, you moron. His parents meant so much to him, he could not afford to feel their loss. The dog he could feel, and through the door of that feeling came everything else." '

The figurative loss of 'my' children and the loss of my cat were minor compared to what my father lost. That is why it was a merciful loss; it was enough to give me a taste of what my father felt, and a taste was all I could bear. I had not understood this before. The family myth was that my father was weak, neurotic, a little boy unable to emotionally grow up. There was some reality to this perception. But the bigger reality is this: my father was strong, much stronger than I am. If I had experienced what he had experienced by the age of nine, it would've broken me several times over. What happened to him hurt him, and badly. It did not break him. He raised a family and held a job. He was brutally unhappy and sometimes he behaved cruelly and contemptibly towards his wife and children. But he never stopped. He never broke. Until the very end.

Caesar once asked me if he could come live with us. I said I didn't think he really wanted that; for one thing, we would make him do his homework constantly. He replied that he would. I said I thought he would miss his mother too much. He hesitated, then replied that maybe he would. I said, 'Besides, we wouldn't hit you when you were bad, and then you wouldn't know what to do.'

He was silent for a moment. Then he said, 'You're right.'

'Why do you think that is?' I asked.

He thought for a long time; I could tell that he was thinking hard. 'I don't know. Why do *you* think that is?'

'Honey,' I said, 'I don't know the answer to that. Nobody knows the answer to that. If you could answer that, you would make a million dollars.'

Maybe it was a strange conversation to have with a ten-year-old. But I wanted him to think about it even if he would never find the answer. If he could think about why he needed to be hit, then he would know that the need to be hit wasn't *him*, but something separate, about which he might have thoughts. I'm not sure this would make any difference. Once, during a fight with him about his throwing rocks at some ducks, I said, 'Do you want me to treat you like that, just because I'm bigger? Do you want me to hit you?'

He said, 'Yeah, hit me, go on.' He said it a couple of times.

I didn't. I turned and walked away. But for a moment I was tempted. I was tempted partly by frustration. I was also tempted by the force of his need.

These children, you see, were not weak people. They were troubled, at risk, disadvantaged, they suffered from low self-esteem – anything you like. Socially, I was their superior in every way. But in a bigger, harder to articulate way, they were at least my equals. It is possible that in some ways they were stronger. Sometimes, when Natalia and I were watching a movie together, she would lean against my shoulder and I would acutely feel that my smaller body, my bony shoulder, were not big enough to bear her weight. I would feel, I am simply not big enough to give this girl what she needs. I had moments of great joy with them; watching them unwrap their presents under the Christmas tree, making them sandwiches, watching Natalia on a horse or Caesar learning how to swim. But I often felt inadequate, wrong, unable to affect them, frustrated, mismatched – at best like a well-intentioned mouse crazily trying to chew two bear cubs out of a massive double net cast upon them by powers beyond its tiny vision.

They knew this, I'm sure. They no doubt sometimes felt scorn for my feelings of ineptitude, and also for my attempts to act confident in spite of them, to be inspiring and optimistic when I barely knew how. But they were also supportive and, on occasion, very kind. When me or Peter were trying to do something and it wasn't working out easily – put dinner on the table, find the petting zoo, get our erratic VCR to play – the kids would sometimes get very quiet and we could feel them unite in their appreciation of our efforts, subtly throwing their good will behind us. Sometimes, I felt their generosity even when they weren't there, as if they were standing behind me, their hands on my shoulders. I am afraid of flying, and I remember one panic-stricken moment at an airport, when my own mind became too much for me to bear; the only way for me to calm myself was to remember Natalia riding a horse, sitting up straight in the saddle and smiling.

After Gattino had been gone almost two months, I visited a woman whose husband had died three years earlier. She was still deep in grief, and her grief accentuated her propensity for mysticism; to her I wondered if the blue marble which had so magically appeared to me in Italy, and which I then threw away, might have something to do with the cat's disappearance. Instead of trying to talk common sense to me, the grieving woman said she knew of a great psychic who might be able to answer that question. I said, no, I did not want to pay any more psychics. The woman said that this psychic was a friend of hers, and that she would just ask her the question, that it need not be a full reading.

A few weeks later I received an email from this psychic which said that the blue marble was not a curse or an omen of any kind. However, its physical movement across the floor had been the by-product of a deliberate psychic energy directed towards me by a young man at Santa Maddalena; this young man was a practitioner of magic, and he had recognized me as a kindred spirit, a person in need of love and capable of fully expressed love. He had wished me well, and it was the force of his wish that had set the marble rolling. It had nothing to do with Gattino, but became bound up with the circumstances of the cat, which was interesting to the psychic because the marble was to her symbolic of an eye, and the kitten was missing an eye.

She added that Gattino was not dead; she said that he had been picked up by a 'traveller' who was well acquainted with the system of cat shelters and havens all over the state. This traveller had taken my cat to one of these shelters, where he was at this moment being well cared for. If I wanted to find him, she suggested that I contact every such shelter within a fifty-mile radius.

This information would, she said, cost me one hundred dollars.

If someone had told me to smear shit on myself and roll in the yard, if that person was a cat expert and made a convincing case that, yes, doing so *could* result in the return of my cat, I probably would've done it. I did not consider this pathetic susceptibility 'magical thinking'. I didn't consider it very different from any other kind of thinking. It was more that the known, visible order of things had become unacceptable to me – senseless, actually – because it was too violently at odds with the needs of my disordered mind. Other kinds of order began to become visible to me, to bleed through and knit together the broken order of what had previously been known. I still don't know if this cobbled reality was completely illusory, an act of desperate will – or if it was an inept and partial interpretation of something real, something bigger than what I could readily see. In this way my connective symbols – the marble, the things different psychics said to me – were similar to religious statues and icons that people pray to, or parade through the street with, or wear around their necks. Except that the statues and icons are also artful creations, sometimes beautiful ones. My symbols were not beautiful, they were stupid and trite. They were related to the symbols of religion as a deformed and retarded child might be the distant cousin of a beautiful prince. But they were related nonetheless.

I paid the money. I called, and Peter helped me call, all the cat shelters within a fifty-mile radius. Many of the shelters I contacted asked me to send them a picture of Gattino along with my contact information which they posted on their Internet sites; I immediately began getting responses from people who thought they might've seen him. I also got responses from businesses devoted to the rescue of hopelessly lost cats, including a private detective willing to fly to your state with his tracking dogs, a smiling pit bull and a vigilant poodle depicted on the company's website nobly flanking their owner. The superior quality of these businesses was attested to by customer after satisfied customer on each of the sites: 'At first I was skeptical. But as soon as I opened my front door and saw Butch and his gentle tracking dogs, I knew...'

I also received an email from someone who appeared barely able to write English, but who claimed to have seen someone named 'Samuel' find a cat outside of a 'community center', to have talked with Samuel about seeing an ad for my cat online and to have gotten an email address from Samuel, if I wanted to contact him. 'Samuel' of course wanted to see a picture of Gattino to be sure he had the right cat; on receiving a photo he said that yes, he definitely had my cat. He went on to say that, like me, he had fallen in love with Gattino and taken him home to Nigeria, but if only I would send the airfare, he would return my darling. Upon Googling the first few lines of 'Samuel's' note, I found an outraged warning about him from someone who had paid the fee and never saw her cat.

★

This is Leslie Fiedler, writing about Simone Weil.

> This world is the only reality available to us, and if we do not love it in all its terror, we are sure to end up loving the 'imaginary,' our own dreams and self-deceits, the utopias of politicians, or the futile promises of future reward and consolation which the misled blasphemously call 'religion.'

When I read it I thought, yes, that is me: deep in dreams of marbles, omens and psychics, hoping that something will have pity on me and my cat. But can one always tell what is imaginary and what isn't? To be 'sentimental' is scorned by intelligent people as false, but the word is one short syllable away from 'sentiment', that is, feeling. False feeling is so blended with real feeling in human life, I wonder if anyone can always tell them apart, or know when one may be hiding in the other. When my father was dying he cried out for people who were not there, in a voice that we did not recognize as his. One of these times he said, 'I want my mama.' When we heard this, Jane and I froze; both of us were asking ourselves, should we pretend to be his mother? It was Martha who knew what to do; she held his hand and sang to him. She sang him a lullaby, and he calmed. He thought his mother was there. Was this a dream, a self-deceit?

I called the three young men who had been at or near Santa Maddalena with me, to find out if any of them practised magic. The first one I called was a medical student who had also written an internationally acclaimed book about a child soldier in West Africa. I emailed him first and asked if we could talk on the phone. He could scarcely have imagined what was coming: 'I know this is a peculiar question,' I asked, 'but do you practise anything that anyone could call magic?'

There was a long silence. 'Do you mean literally?' he asked.

I thought about it. 'Yes,' I said. 'I think I do.'

The silence that followed was so baffled that I broke down and explained why I was asking.

'Well,' he said, 'I pray. Do you think that counts?'

I said, 'To me it could. But I don't think that's what the lady meant.'
He was very sympathetic about Gattino. He said he would pray for
me to find him. I thanked him and called someone else.

When my father was alive, he and Martha were distant,
uncomprehending, nearly hostile. He was cold to her, and she felt
rejected by him. As he became more and more unhappy with age and
was eventually rejected by my mother, he tried to reach out to Martha.
But the pattern was too set. During one of our last Christmas visits to
him, I saw my father and Martha act out a scene which looked like a
strange imitation of a cruel game between a girl who is madly in love
with an indifferent boy, and the boy himself. She kept asking him over
and over again, did he like the present she had gotten him? Did he
really, really like it? Would he use it? Did he want to try it out now? And
he responded stiffly, irritably, with increasing distance. She behaved as
if she wanted to win his love, but she was playing the loser so
aggressively that it was almost impossible for him to respond with love,
or to respond at all. What was the real feeling here? What was the
dream or the self-deceit? Something real was happening, and it was
terrible to see. But it was so disguised that it is hard to say what it
actually was.

Still, as he lay dying, she was the one who knew to hold his hand;
to sing to him.

The second young man I called, a Hungarian writer I had met outside
of Santa Maddalena, answered quite differently from the first. 'I have
powers,' he said intensely, 'but I have never been taught how to use
them very well. If I made something move, it would be something big,
like a building. But a marble – I'm not that good. To move something
that small would require more refinement than I possess.'

At least this conversation made me smile; when I repeated it at a
party, I meant to amuse people – but it actually offended someone. 'He
sounds like an idiot!' said a film producer who happened to overhear
me. 'There's nothing charming in that, he just sounds really, really

stupid.' And then the producer, the voice of normalcy and intelligence, began describing to me his latest idea for a comedy: A man who married very young is, at thirty, full of wanderlust. His wife goes off for a trip alone, and he finds himself in the presence of a beautiful young woman who wants him. 'Finally, she gets him alone and she takes off her shirt, and she's got incredible tits, really big tits, and they're perfect, the most beautiful big tits you've ever seen! But he says no and—'

I laughed, almost hysterically. Yes, it was a comedy, and a deeper one than its creator knew, to have at its dramatic centre the rejection of beautiful naked breasts. Of course the hero rejects these breasts in the name of faithfulness, and rationally all is well. But if one mutes the trite music of the story and watches the action as sketched by the producer, one sees a different, more stark play. Whether it's a comedy or a drama, a titillating image or a perverse one, depends on what you feel about naked breasts, which in the most fundamental symbolic language, translate as nurture, love and vulnerability.

My sister was offering my father love, in a form he could not accept, just as he, with increasing desperation, offered my mother love she could not accept or even recognize. In each offering, purity and perversity made a strange pattern; each rejection made the pattern more complete.

If my father had acted differently towards Martha, it is possible that he could've broken this pattern. Because he was the parent, it's possible that the burden was on him to do so. But I don't think he could. He wasn't sophisticated when it came to his emotions. His emotions were too raw for sophistication.

When I was thirty-two, I tried to break the pattern. I was visiting home and my father was having a temper tantrum, which meant on this occasion that he was yelling at my mother about her failings. He had done this for years, and normally the entire family would be silent and wait for him to tire himself out. This time I did not. I yelled at him. I told him I was sick of listening to him complain and blame everything on someone else. I expected him to yell back at me; in the past, I might've expected him to hit me. But he didn't. He turned and walked away. I followed him, still yelling. Finally I yelled, 'I am sorry for talking to you this way. I'm doing it because I want to have a real relationship with you. Do you want a real relationship with me?'

He said, 'No,' and shut his bedroom door in my face.

I felt bad. I also felt vindicated. I had been right and he had been wrong. Even so, I apologized the next day, and we talked, a little. He did not take back his words. That made me even more right. It made me right to emotionally shut the door on him.

I repeated this conversation to an older man, a friend who is also a father. He laughed and said, 'I would've said "no" too if I were him.'

I asked why. I don't remember what he said. I came away with the impression that my friend found the language I used too corny or therapeutic. And it was. Certainly my father would've found it so. But I don't think that's the only reason he walked away. If my language was a cliché, it was also heartfelt and naked. That kind of sudden nakedness, without even a posture of elegance, would've been a kind of violence to my father. It would've touched him forcefully in a place he had spent his life guarding. To say 'yes' would've allowed too much of that force in too deeply. Saying 'no' was a way of being faithful to the guarded place.

My father continued to throw tantrums and blame people for his suffering. A little while after I asked him if he wanted a real relationship with me, I wrote a letter telling him how angry I was with him for acting that way. Before I sent it, I told my mother about it. She said it would really hurt him. She said, 'He told me, "Mary and I have a real relationship." ' At the time I thought, how sad. Now I think he was right. Our relationship was real. What I wanted it to be was ideal.

Because a security guard named Gino claimed to have seen Gattino months after he disappeared, both Peter and I began to believe that he had somehow found a place to survive, even though the temperatures had sometimes gone down to freezing, even though it must've been hard to get enough to eat. I began draping the bushes of our house with sweaty clothes, hoping that the wind would carry the scent to him and that he would be able to find his way back. We continued to put food out in sheltered places near parking areas; in addition, we began to 'stake out' these areas almost every night, sitting in our car with the headlights trained on the food. We saw at least two cats come to eat – both were grey tabbies, but big ones that surely no one could mistake for the delicate cat depicted on our poster. Only once, Peter saw a very small, thin cat who could've been ours, but he couldn't get a good look because it was slinking under parked cars. It was about to emerge into the open when a noisy crowd of students came by and it darted away back under the cars.

The very act of doing these things – waiting in the parking lots, draping the bushes with clothing – made me feel that Gattino was still there.

Before I met Gattino, before I went to Italy, I talked with Caesar on the phone, and during that conversation he asked why I sent his mother money. I could have said, because I love you and I want to help her take care of you. Instead I said, 'Because when I first met your mother and she told me she made six dollars and forty cents an hour, I felt ashamed as an American. I felt like she deserved more support for coming here and trying to get a better life.'

He said, 'What you're saying is really fucked up.'

I said, 'Why?'

He said, 'I don't know, it just is.'

I said, 'Put words on it. Try.'

He said, 'I can't.'

I said, 'Yes, you can. Why is what I'm saying fucked up?'

He said, 'Because it's good enough that she came here to get a better life.'

I said, 'I agree. But she should be acknowledged. I have a hard job and sometimes I hate it, but I get acknowledged and she should too. And somebody besides me should do it, but nobody is, so I am.'

He said, 'People are acknowledging her. She makes more money now.'

I said, 'That's good. But it still should be more.'

He said, 'You act like you feel sorry for her.'

I said, 'I do. So what? Sometimes I feel sorry for Peter, sometimes I feel sorry for myself. There's no shame in that.'

He said, 'But you talk about my mom like she's some kind of freak.'

I said, 'I don't think that.'

He said, 'You talk about her like you think you're better than her.'

And for a moment I was silent. Because I do think that – rather, I feel it. Before God, as souls, I don't feel it. But socially, as creatures of this earth, I do. I'm wrong to feel it. But I do feel it. I feel it partly because of things Caesar and Natalia have told me.

He heard my hesitation and he began to cry. And I so I lied to him. Of course he knew I lied.

He said, 'For the first time I feel ashamed of my family.'

I said I was sorry; I tried to reassure him. He asked me if I would take money from someone who thought they were better than me and I said, 'Frankly, yes. If I needed the money I would take as much as I could, and I would say to myself, "Fuck you for thinking you're better than me." '

Passionately, he said he would never, ever do that.

I snapped, 'Don't be so sure about that. You don't know yet.'

He stopped crying.

I said, 'Caesar, this is really hard. Do you think we can get through it?'

He said, 'I don't know.' Then, 'Yes.'

I asked him if he remembered the time on the train when he was only seven, when he asked me why I loved him and I said I didn't know yet. 'Now I know why,' I said. 'This is why. You're not somebody who just wants to hear nice bullshit. You care. You want to know what's real. I love you for that.'

This was true. But sometimes the truth is too sad to behold. He said he was sorry he'd bothered me, and that he was tired. I asked him if he still felt mad at me. He hesitated and then said, 'No. Inside, I am not mad at you, Mary.'

For months after Gattino disappeared, I still dreamed of him at least once a week. I would dream that I was standing in the yard calling him, like I had before he'd disappeared, and he'd come to me the way he had come in reality: running with his tail up, leaping slightly in his eagerness, leaping finally into my lap. Often in the dream he didn't look like himself; often I blended him with other cats I have had in the past. In one dream I blended him with Caesar. In this dream, Caesar and I were having an argument, and I got so angry I opened my mouth, threatening to bite him. He opened his mouth too, in counter-threat. And when he did that, I saw that he had the small, sharp teeth of a kitten.

When we came back from Italy, Caesar came to visit. We were tired and packing to move. We did not have as much energy as we usually have for him; he felt that immediately and resented it. He said, 'You've changed.' And he became volatile and hostile, behaviour which had a very different quality at the age of twelve than it had when he was seven. The second day he was with us he told Peter, 'I want to cut off your nuts'; I thought Peter would knock him down the stairs. Some days later he told me I didn't have any kids because I went to the vet and 'got fixed'; I answered rationally, but inside, for the first time, my feelings for him went dead.

That night after he went to bed, he started screaming that he couldn't breathe. I gave him his inhaler and rubbed his chest. For over an hour he continued to scream and to force himself to cough, loudly and dramatically. I went in the room and sat with him. I told him I knew he was faking the asthma, and that I also knew it was hard to be with us and that the visit wasn't going right. I told him I was having a hard time sleeping too and that I was really tired, which was part of why I couldn't be as present as I'd like. I put my hand on his stomach and told him to breathe there. He did. We talked about the Harry Potter movie we had seen the night before. We talked about the idea of an alternate universe, and what might be going on in it right now. I felt connected to him again. He closed his eyes and began to breathe evenly. I left his room at one o'clock. He woke me up at six the next morning, demanding that I get up and help him turn on the shower.

In March, four months after Gattino disappeared, I got a call at three a.m. from Gino the security guard who said he had just seen him in one of the parking lots. I put my coat on over my pyjamas, got in the car and was there within minutes. Gino and another guard were excitedly pacing around with flashlights, pointing at the dim figure of a cat under the last car at the end of a row of cars. When I appeared the cat bolted.

'There he goes!' cried Gino. And he shone his flashlight on the obese tabby we had been seeing for months.

'That can't be him,' said the other guard. 'That cat has two eyes.'

'No he doesn't!' insisted Gino. 'I shined my light on him and I saw!'

A few nights later I spoke to another security guard, a reticent older man who had once told me that he'd seen my cat. I asked him, when had he last seen Gattino? He said it had been three months ago – maybe longer. 'I haven't seen many cats lately,' he said. 'I'll tell you what I have seen though. There's a huge bobcat, all over campus late at night. That and a lot of coyotes.'

His meaning was clear. I didn't say much of anything. I thought, at least it's a death an animal would understand.

Caesar did not behave badly the whole visit. He loved Gattino; he loved the story of his illness and his dramatic flight from Italy. When he knew that a friend of Peter's was coming for dinner, he spontaneously spent his own money to buy four cannolis at a pastry shop at which we'd stopped to buy a soda. 'I want to go all out for us,' he said. When it came time to have the dessert, he said, 'Wait, let me get it ready!' And he served the pastry garnished with blueberries, which must've been a last-minute inspiration. But when Peter's friend emailed him a poem to thank him for the cannoli, his response was, 'What a stupid bitch.

What kind of stupid bitch would write this for someone she doesn't even know?' His school had assigned him three book reports over the summer and he hadn't done any. I knew he had read a simplified version of *Call of the Wild* and I knew he had loved it. So I made him write a book report about it. He moaned, 'Aw, man...' But he worked on it for nearly an hour. When he finished I went over it and pointed out the errors, and the places where he needed to be clearer or more specific. He spent at least a half-hour revising it. He showed it to me proudly, and rightly so – it was excellent. A month later I learned that he never turned it in.

I talked to Natalia after Caesar's visit; she asked how it went. I said I was angry at him for not turning in his homework. There was a beat of silence on her end, and then she said, 'I would be mad too.' She said it with a slight smile in her voice. It was two kinds of smile in one: mocking and relieved at having a conventional adult response to mock. She may also have been simply pleased to be on my team for the instant it took to say the sentence; we had not been on the same team for quite a while.

Because Natalia had run away from home repeatedly, she had been sent to live in a group home; she was deemed too wild for foster care. She had been there for two years. The first year she was there, we had managed to get her once more into the camp she had loved, and we had hope that it would work out better now that she wasn't living with her mother. At first, it seemed to. Again the counsellors got excited about her; again she was accepted into the Teen Leadership programme. After a few months, she blew it off. She started going AWOL, skipping school and running the streets. Every weekend, she went home to stay with her mother, even though they fought violently.

Finally her mother said that if Natalia behaved herself for three months straight, stopped violating curfew and went to school, she could return home. Natalia did it, for the entire three months. The court date was set. It was expected to be a walk-through. Formally, the judge asked Natalia's mother if she would allow her to return home.

And her mother laughed. She laughed and said, 'I would never let that girl come live with me again.' The social worker told me Natalia screamed like an animal. She said she had to be held back by court officers. She said that Caesar had been there and that he had laughed along with his mother. She said she had never seen anything like it.

The social worker who told me what happened in court repeated to me what she had said to Natalia: that she 'has to accept her mother for what she is because she will never change'. What heavy knowledge for a young girl. If Natalia actually absorbed such deep knowledge at fifteen – and I suspect that she absorbed it much younger – how can the more refined knowledge of reading and writing and math problems ever seem like anything but trivial to her? What will it do to her to accept a woman who mistreats her? She is sixteen now, and she is finally about to be transferred to a foster home. She still goes back to stay with her mother every weekend. She will go back there again and again. My guess is that she will continue to do so in some form long after her mother is gone.

How stupid to think I could break this pattern when I could not break my own. During the decades before I got married, I can't offhand say how many times I've asked for or demanded some sort of relationship with someone who shut the door in my face, then opened it again and peeked out. I would – metaphorically – pound on the door and follow the person through endless rooms. At least a few times the door opened and I fell in love – before losing interest completely. I thought then that my feelings were false and had been all along – but the pain that came from rejecting or being rejected was real and deep. It did not help when I realized that I was as much or more to blame for the result as the people I pursued, that I often 'played the loser' so aggressively that I scarce gave the person opposite me much choice in their response.

When I talk about my relationship with the children and how frustrating it is, some people say, 'But you're showing them another way.' Am I? Deeper than my encouraging, ideal words is my experience of the closed door and the desperate insistence that it open

– emotional absence, followed by a compulsive reaction that becomes its own kind of absence. Even if they don't identify it, I'm sure the children feel it.

I'm also sure that they feel the true, live thing trapped somehow inside the false game – if in fact 'game' is the right word for what I have described. A game is something conscious, with clear rules and goals that everyone agrees to. What I experienced too often, inside myself or with another, was a half-conscious, fast-moving blur of real and false, playfulness and anguish, ardent affection and its utter lack. More than a game, it was as if I were stumbling, with another person or alone, through a labyrinth of conflicting impulses and complex, overlaid patterns, trying to find a way to meet, or to avoid meeting, both at the same time. In spite of everything, sometimes I did meet with people, and lovingly. I met my husband in that way almost by accident. And sometimes, after ten years, he and I nonetheless find ourselves wandering apart and alone.

And so I take the kids to movies and to plays; I send them books, listen to them talk, and lecture them about their homework, still sometimes try to help them do it. I dedicated a book to Natalia and sent it to her so she could see her name written in it. I don't think I will ever fully know how any of these actions affect her or Caesar, for good or ill. I act almost blindly and hope that most of it will be to the good.

This too my father experienced.

When I was about forty, my father called me to tell me that he had found a picture that I had drawn when I was seven, and that it 'showed real talent'. He said that he had planned to frame it but then he lost it; he looked everywhere, he was frantic. Then he realized it could've gotten mixed up with some magazines that he had taken to a recycling bin – he went to the bin, which was full of sticky crap and swarmed by bees, and he spent at least an hour looking for the picture. He didn't find it. But now, a month later, he had discovered it under another pile of papers. He was happy and relieved and he wanted me to know.

*

I don't remember how I reacted. I remember that the tone of his words was the same to me as if he had called to once again announce that he was going to kill himself, or to try to persuade me to talk our mother into coming back to him, or to tell me that having children had ruined his life, or to rage about the noise a neighbour was making.

The family myth was that our father was crazy, compulsive, obsessed with things like bargains on toilet paper or coupons. And he was. It was hard to hear feeling in his words because his voice and his words were habitually agitated, obsessed, so tight that the feeling of them was lost.

After he died I found the drawing he was talking about. It was framed and hanging on his wall; I must've seen it before when I'd come to visit. But I had not registered it. My feelings had become as lost as his had been. I sat with the picture and cried.

At the end of Caesar's last visit we drove him back to the city. While I thought he was asleep in the back seat, I had a conversation with Peter about human love, how perverted and cruel it can be on the one hand, how bluntly, functionally biological on the other. Flippantly I said, 'Maybe it actually doesn't even exist.' Right after I said that, a stuffed animal bounced off my head and into my lap; it was a smiling little cow that Caesar had won for me at the county fair the previous day. 'What do you call that?' he asked. I laughed and thanked him.

Love as a cheap stuffed toy bounced off your head – it's a brilliant metaphor and a true one. But the metaphor for love that I feel more deeply is a lost, hungry little animal dying as it tries to find its way back home in the cold. It isn't truer. But I feel it more.

Maybe, though, it is wrong to put the weight of such a metaphor on to the memory of something so small and light as a kitten. Maybe it was wrong to chase my father through his house shouting about 'a real relationship'; maybe it is even worse to keep analysing and questioning what his experience was and what it meant, in public no less. It was certainly wrong to use people to repeatedly replay this drama, whether they willingly participated or not, whether I knew what

I was doing or not. It may be wrong to feel like I have 'lost' Caesar and Natalia because they aren't doing what I want them to do. It's also possible that if they choose to hurt themselves by deliberately failing and rejecting much of what I can give them I *should* lose them; I'm not sure.

I once read a Chekhov story which described a minor character as 'trying to snatch from life more than it can give'; maybe I have turned into such a person, unable to accept what is given, always trying to tear things up in order to find what is 'real', even when I don't know what 'real' is, unable to maintain the respect, the dignity of not asking too much or even looking too closely at the workings of the heart, which, no matter how you look, can never be fully seen or understood.

The thought makes me look down in self-reproach. Then I think, but life can give a lot. If you can't see inside the heart no matter how you look, then why not look? Why not see as much as you can? How is that disrespectful? If you are only given one look, shouldn't you look as fully as you can? A lost cat would not ask itself if food and shelter were too much to expect, or try to figure out how much food and shelter were enough or who was the right person to give those things. It would just keep trying to get those things until the moment it died.

During the time I was beginning to lose hope of finding Gattino I went to Montana to do a reading at a university there. My hotel room overlooked a river, and one day as I was staring out the window, some people with a dog came walking along the riverbank. The dog got excited, and his owner let him off his chain. He went running and made a wild leap into the water, his legs splayed ecstatically wide. I smiled and thought 'Gattino'; for once the thought was comforting, not sad. I thought, even if he is dead, he's still here in that splayed, ecstatic leap.

This idea was no doubt an illusion, a self-deception. But that dog was not. That dog was real. And so was Gattino. ■

THE ENCIRCLEMENT

Tamas Dobozy

At some point during the lecture Sándor would get up, point a finger at Professor Teleki and accuse him of lying – and Teleki would gasp and sputter and grow red in the face and the audience would love it. But it wasn't an act, and Teleki had approached Sándor many times – either personally or through his agent – to ask what his problem was. He even offered him money, which Sándor accepted, only to break his promise and show up at the lectures again – to the point where audiences started expecting him, as if Teleki's presence was secondary, playing the straight man to this hectoring, vindictive blind guy who was the star of the show.

Yes, Sándor was blind. Which only made it more incredible, especially in the early days, that he'd managed to follow Teleki all over North America, from one stop on the lecture circuit to the next. 'How the hell can a blind man,' Teleki yelled at his agent, 'get around the country so quickly?' Nonetheless, Teleki could see it: Sándor in a dark overcoat, black glasses not flashing in the sunshine so much as absorbing it, his cane tip-tapping along the pavement through all kinds of landscape

– deserts, mountains, prairies – and weather – squalls, blizzards, heatwaves – aimed directly at the place where Teleki had scheduled his next appearance. It was like something out of a bad folktale.

But once Teleki started bribing him the vision changed, and he always pictured Sándor sipping mai tais in the airport lounge before boarding with the first-class ticket Teleki's hush money had bought him, chatting amiably with businessmen and flirting, in a blind-man sort of way, with the stewardesses, though this was as far from the truth as the first vision had been, as Sándor himself explained.

They sat in the bar of the Seelbach Hilton in Louisville and Sándor, with a casual seriousness that always drove Teleki crazy, told him he hadn't spent a cent Teleki had given him and that every single trip had been accomplished through the 'assistance of strangers'. All he had to do, Sándor said, was step out the door and instantly there were people there, asking if he was okay, if there was anything they could do to help, if there was something he needed. When Teleki said he found it hard to believe that such spontaneous charity could have gotten him from Toronto to New York, to Montreal, Halifax, Boston, Chicago, Calgary, Los Angeles, Vancouver and Anchorage, in that order, on time for every single one of his lectures, Sándor replied, 'You can believe it or not, but that's exactly what happened.' He'd found out about Teleki's itinerary, grabbed his coat and suitcase and cane, and walked out of the door into the care of the first stranger he'd met, and from there, 'Well, things took care of themselves.' Teleki looked at him, then around the Seelbach, wondering if he could get away with strangling Sándor right there.

The point at which Sándor would usually rise from his seat – various people supporting him by the elbows – was when Teleki began to describe the morning of January 18, 1945 in Budapest, the minute he'd stepped off the Chain Bridge, and the order went out to blow it up, along with the Hungarian and German soldiers, the peasants and their wheelbarrows full of ducks, the middle-class children and women and men, suitcases packed, still streaming across it. By then, the bridges

were a tangled mass of metal, holes gaping along the causeway, cars
stuck in them, on fire, bodies shredded by Soviet artillery and tangled
in the cables and railings, thousands of people trying to force their way
across in advance of the Soviets, trampling and being trampled on,
cursing in the near dark, forced over the sides into the icy river, mowed
down by fighter planes, Red Army tanks, machine guns, while behind
their backs, in that half of Budapest, the siege went on, fighting from
street to street, building to building, the whole place ablaze.

'Tell them how you grabbed two of the children whose parents had
died coming across the bridge,' Sándor would yell at him at this point.
'Tell them how you held them to your chest, telling the Arrow Cross
officer you couldn't join the siege effort because your wife had just
died. And then tell them how you abandoned those kids in the next
street. You tell them that!' Sándor jabbed his cane in Teleki's direction.

'That never happened!' Teleki would shout back. 'I never did that.'

And the audience would hoot and laugh and clap, egging Sándor on.

It was always something different, another aspect of the story
sabotaged. When Teleki got to the part about how he'd gone up to the
castle and 'volunteered', as he put it, to join the defence under
Lieutenant-Colonel László Veresváry, Sándor stood up – someone had
handed him a bullhorn – and did a high-pitched imitation of how
Teleki, after abandoning the children, had run into an Arrow Cross
soldier who saw that he was able-bodied and told him to get up to the
castle. 'B-b-b-b-but, I'm just looking for foooooood,' whined Sándor. 'I-
I-I-I left my kids a block over and I was about to go back for them. My
wife, you see, she died when they blew up the bridge...' And here
Sándor fell into a fit of such flawless mock weeping that many in the
audience turned towards Teleki and copied him. 'But the soldier forced
you up to the castle anyhow, didn't he?' said Sándor, suddenly serious.
'Giving your ass a kick every few feet just to make sure you got there.'

'I have no idea what you're talking about,' said Teleki, trying to look
cool. 'And if you don't stop interrupting my talks I'm going to have a
restraining order put on you.'

But Teleki's agent advised him against this. How would it look, he asked, if Teleki, the great professor of twentieth-century Middle European history, award-winning author of biographies and memoirs, survivor of the siege of Budapest, were suddenly afraid of the rantings of a blind man? Besides, as the agent had explained, it would only provide more publicity for Sándor, which was the last thing either of them wanted. He finally suggested – and he was surprised that Teleki hadn't considered this himself – that he get his act together and take on Sándor directly, since he was after all a historian. Or was he?

Teleki looked at him, wondering whether his agent had been to one of his lectures lately. Had he seen what went on up there? Sándor was killing him, and on the very ground where Teleki was supposed to be the authority. On the other hand, looking again at his agent, Teleki realized that maybe he didn't want him to get rid of Sándor, that maybe – no, *probably* – his agent was actually happy with the way things were working out, eagerly calculating his percentage from the recent 'bump' in ticket sales.

'What I mean,' said the agent, 'is find out who this Sándor guy is. Isn't that something you do? Root around in people's pasts?'

Teleki had not known how to respond to that. Sándor Veselényi was his name; that's as far as they'd gotten during their first few meetings. And he couldn't just walk into the nearest archive and pull out the file with that name and voila, there would be everything from the baptismal record through to the accident that caused his blindness to why he'd decided to make it his life's work to humiliate Teleki. No, it would take years to do that kind of research, just as it had taken years to gather material for each of the biographies and memoirs Teleki had written, to put together the lecture that was now, unfortunately, thrilling audiences more than ever, and which he was contractually locked into.

Not that it wouldn't have been nice – Teleki was the first to admit – to get up at the lectern and to lay it all out the next time Sándor opened his mouth, flashing the slides of Sándor in his fascist uniform, a member of the Arrow Cross, or better yet of Father Kun's murderous band, so unlike the Germans in their rejection of efficiency, in really going out of their way, even to be inconvenienced, as long as it meant slaughtering the Jews *just right*. And for the coup de grâce, for a nice moral twist at the end of the story, something about how Sándor had been blinded by his own desire to seek and destroy, perhaps a shard of glass from an explosion he'd rigged in one of the buildings in the Budapest ghetto – whole families tied up inside.

But Teleki had no information on Sándor – only on himself. He'd get up there with his black-and-white slides, his laser pointer, his tongue tripping up, bogged down, boxed in by English, a language so clunky compared to his own, and try to tighten up his story even further, to make himself appear even *more* authentic, only to have Sándor hobble in on the arms of two businessmen, a mother of three, four old men in outdated suits and two guys sporting Mohawks.

Teleki spoke on, trying to keep his voice from going falsetto. He focused on the crowd – the usual assemblage of academics, writers, journalists, immigrants, students, amateur historians, senior citizens – and pointed to the picture of himself in the uniform of Veresváry's garrison, expected to keep the Soviets from capturing Buda castle, where the SS and Arrow Cross commanders were wringing their hands in the middle of the siege, encircled entirely by the Red Army, trying to figure out what to do. At night, young men, really just boys, would try to fly in supplies by glider, Soviet artillery shooting them out of the sky. Teleki struck a solemn tone when he told the crowd that the place they were supposed to land – Vérmező – could be translated as 'Blood Meadow'.

When Sándor stayed silent, Teleki grew braver, and he told them of what it was like in the final days of the siege, the desperate order of the castle with its German and Hungarian armies, the soldiers too frightened of punishment – usually a bullet in the head – to voice what was on their minds: why SS Obergruppenführer Pfeffer-Wildenbruch hadn't gotten them the hell out of Budapest, why they were clearly sitting around waiting to be slaughtered. Worse still was being under the command of Veresváry, whose soldiers were men like Teleki –

refugees or criminals or labourers pressed into service – for whom Veresváry was always willing to spare a bit of whipping from the riding crop he carried around, brandishing it over his head as he strode along the trenches they'd dug and were defending, as if the Soviet bullets whizzing around him were so many mosquitoes. Veresváry would sentence men to death for cowardice, then commute the sentence, then brutalize them so badly over the next several days – screaming and kicking at them while the fusillade continued, a horizontal rain of bullets and mortars – that the men would eventually stand in the trench, ostensibly to take better aim at the enemy, though from the way their guns hung in their hands it was little more than suicide. They stood there until half their faces suddenly vanished in a splatter, or their backs bloomed open, red and purple and bone. This seemed to satisfy Veresváry, who praised them as they fell, pointing to how they slumped, knees buckling, heads thrown back, and said to the rest, 'There was a soldier, you chickenshits. There was a soldier!'

'Was that why you came up with the plan to do away with him? To undermine and to betray and to murder your commander?' asked Sándor, standing up.

'You must be thinking of someone else, Sándor.'

'Sure you did. You went from soldier to soldier and then, when you had them on side, you turned around and betrayed them to Pfeffer-Wildenbruch, telling him you'd heard whispers that there would be a mutiny.'

'That's the biggest lie I've ever…'

'Look at the next picture. Look at it.'

The audience turned from Sándor to Teleki, who was standing there, mouth agape, the remote control in hand, his finger poised above the button, wondering whether Sándor was bluffing, or whether he'd somehow managed to hijack the projector, slipping in a different set of slides.

'Let's see it,' someone in the audience yelled, and everyone laughed.

Teleki hit the button and there they were: all those arrested on charges of treason, five battered men with rotting clothes and unshaven faces standing against the blackened walls of the castle district, loosely grouped together, as if they were not yet accused and looking to slink off before it happened. It was the picture as Teleki remembered it, in exactly the place where it always appeared.

'There you are. You're standing just to the left of Pfeffer-Wildenbruch. That's you right there, you dirty stinking fink! You sold out all your comrades!'

Teleki turned, squinting at the photograph, noting with eye-opening surprise that the guy there did resemble, in a way, what he might have looked like thirty years ago, after seventy or so days of siege – malnourished, frightened to death, desperate.

The audience applauded.

'The guy can see photographs!' said Teleki to his agent. 'He's a complete fraud!'

'Why didn't you say anything at the lecture?'

'I did! But nobody could hear me! They were too busy applauding!'

His agent shrugged. 'Maybe he saw the photograph before he went blind. Maybe somebody described it to him.'

'Come off it,' Teleki said.

'So how come he knows so much about you, then?'

'He doesn't know anything about me! All that stuff... he's lying!'

The agent looked at him with a raised eyebrow.

'What? You believe him now, too?'

'The only thing I believe in is sales,' replied the agent, recovering quickly. 'And sales are excellent,' he said. 'How would you feel about playing in bigger venues?'

'I'm not "playing"! I'm trying to inform people, to teach them something!'

What Teleki noticed next was that Sándor's entourage seemed to be growing, as if the people who helped him were no longer dropping him off at the lectures and going on their way, but sticking around, as if something in Sándor's words, the depth of his conviction, had brought them into contact with a higher cause, a belief system. *Great,* thought Teleki. *Just what I need: Sándor becoming a guru.*

In addition, it seemed as though Sándor was now doing more of the talking than Teleki was – bellowing on, jabbing the cane in Teleki's direction, the group of people immediately around him more vociferous in their approval than the rest. By the end of the night, Teleki noted that he'd spoken only three minutes more than Sándor.

But it was not just this that made Teleki decide, then and there, after twelve fingers of Scotch on the balcony of his hotel room, to pack it in, but also what Sándor had said. For the first time since the beginning of their conflict he was seriously doubting whether he knew more about the siege than the blind man, or whether, in fact, his very first guess had been right after all and that Sándor, far from being a disabled person, was some spirit of vengeance, one of those mythic figures who were blind not because they couldn't see, but because they were distracted from the material world by a deeper insight, by being able to peer into secret places. Of course, remembering how he'd seen Sándor walk into pillars or trip over seats, Teleki laughed and dismissed the thought, though it always came back, forcing him up from sleep, the extent of Sándor's information, the way he could retrieve things from the abyss of the past.

For when Teleki had described the last few days in the castle, how Veresváry ordered them to draw up surveillance maps using telescopes taken from the National Archives, plotting the streets in the direction of western Buda, Sándor had nodded in his seat. When Teleki said that rumours of a breakout had been swirling for days, Sándor rose up, but said nothing. Nervously, Teleki had continued, saying the German soldiers, during the Second World War, never surrendered, preferring the death of fighting on, of retreat, rather than captivity, for they'd been told of the horrors and torments of Siberia, as if it was possible to imagine a place where death was salvation.

Teleki was sent to Pfeffer-Wildenbruch with the map they'd drawn up. At this point in the story, Sándor began rubbing his hands together, waiting for Teleki to repeat what Pfeffer-Wildenbruch had said that day as he took the documents from Teleki's hand, staring right through him as if he wasn't in the room, as if there was only the Obergruppenführer himself, alone with the choices he couldn't make.

'If I give the order for a breakout,' he mumbled, 'everyone will die.'

It was here that Sándor finally chimed in, mimicking the reply Teleki was supposed to have given: 'S-s-s-surely not everyone.'

Teleki reached for the volume adjustment on his microphone, continuing with what Pfeffer-Wildenbruch had said to him: 'You'll probably be one of the first to die.'

'I-i-it's a fitting thing, sir,' Sándor interrupted him again.

'I did not say that!' shouted Teleki, turning the volume all the way up.

Someone handed Sándor the bullhorn again. 'To face the enemy directly is a fitting thing, Obergruppenführer, sir. Without flinching.'

Suddenly Sándor began to play both roles, turning this way and that to indicate when Pfeffer-Wildenbruch and when Teleki was speaking, the crowd watching raptly, oblivious to the 'No, no, no!' Teleki was shouting into the microphone.

'Meanwhile,' said Sándor, now in the role of Teleki, 'while the men are proving their bravery, we could do *our* duty and escape using the sewers under the castle.'

'Our duty?' Sándor carried off Pfeffer-Wildenbruch's fatigue perfectly.

'I-i-i-it would not be cowardice,' Sándor stuttered, again playing Teleki. 'Such words belong to narcissists, those who worry for their reputations, for how history will regard them. No' – Sándor shook his head as Teleki might have – 'we must look beyond our egos, our timid wish for glory. The war effort needs us…needs *you*…to survive this. You must sacrifice your pride for the greater good.' Then, in a flourish, Sándor removed his glasses, shifting his eyes from side to side, as Teleki had done so many times behind the lectern. 'Obergruppenführer, sir, I've heard the men speaking of a plot on Lieutenant-Colonel Veresváry's life. In the sewers, you will need men you can trust… To prove my devotion I will give you the names of the conspirators.'

'And so,' Sándor now said, returning to himself (what Teleki increasingly considered the *role* of himself), 'while men died by the thousands in the breakout, our friend here' – he indicated Teleki – 'was splashing through the sewers.'

The sewers. Here, Sándor's knowledge was just as extensive. It was called Ördög-árok, 'Devil's Ditch', a name in keeping with what was to greet them, descending into waters swirling with suitcases, soggy files, fragments of memoranda, whole suits of clothing from which men and women seemed to have dissolved, a wooden statue of the Virgin face down, her hand entwined with the much smaller one of a body trapped in the waters beneath her. They ran into loose bands of SS. They waited below while men tried scaling the rungs of ladders to sewer gratings above, poking their heads out, followed by the crack of a sniper's bullet, the body falling back and knocking off all who were clinging to the ladder.

They entered aqueducts that grew narrower and narrower, Pfeffer-Wildenbruch sending Teleki on ahead (or so Sándor said) into places he could move along crouched over, then only on his hands and knees, and finally on his belly, each pipe he went into smaller than the last, until he was overcome by claustrophobia and panicked, inching backwards on his stomach and chest like some worm reversing itself – only to find that Pfeffer-Wildenbruch and his party had moved on, leaving him behind. It was at this point that he ran into Hungarian commander Ivan Hindy and two soldiers and his wife, still wearing the finery she put on every day, as befitted her position, the hem of her dress drifting out around her as she whispered to the men on either side, trying to keep the mood light, the conversation agreeable, even as the screams of men rang up and down the sewer. They were holding her by both elbows, but it seemed as if she was holding them, especially the soldier whose arm was in a sling, as if the sound of her voice could keep them going, as if in allowing them to hold her she was lending them strength.

As Sándor's story went – and it was a compelling story, Teleki had to admit, so much so that even *he* wanted to hear how it would end – Teleki was reluctant to accept Hindy's order to bring up the rear of their little party. And when Hindy, seeing his reluctance, suggested that he could go to the front then, Teleki again demurred. 'Well, where would you like to be?' And when Teleki said he would prefer to stay in the middle, alongside Mrs Hindy, everyone laughed, their echoes bouncing off the walls and water until he realized they'd stopped caring, that he was trapped in a group of people tripping along cheerily to capture, trial, execution.

'M-m-m-maybe we should try another few of the sewer gratings,' he said, pointing up, waiting for a break in the laughter.

'Would you prefer to go first or second?' Hindy asked, and when Teleki said second they laughed all over again – except for Mrs Hindy, who reached forward (Sándor reproducing her movement for the benefit of the audience) and tenderly stroked Teleki's cheek.

It was decided that the uninjured soldier would go first, since he was the heaviest and would need two men to lift him within reach of the first rung of the ladder. He would see whether there were snipers present, and draw their fire away from the manhole, hopefully without getting his head blown off. Next would come Teleki, whom the commander could boost up alone, and who'd then help, from above, with the delicate job of heaving up the injured soldier, as well as the voluminous Mrs Hindy, and finally Hindy himself.

The soldier nodded, taking a long swig from a bottle of Napoleon brandy he said he'd found floating in the sewer, then stepped on to the hands held out to him and reached for the ladder, crawling up it quickly and pushing open the grating. *Click.* There was the sound of a firing pin hitting a dud cartridge. Looking up, they saw the soldier staring directly into the barrel of a Soviet gun, though in the next second he'd swung the bottle of brandy into the Russian's face, rolled quickly out of the hole and run, the Soviet soldier giving his head a shake and then chasing after him. Within seconds, Hindy was holding out his hands for Teleki, who looked at them, placed his foot tentatively into the knitted fingers, then boosted himself up, only to have Hindy remove them the instant he'd grabbed the rung, leaving him dangling there, too weak to pull himself up and too afraid to fall back into the sewer, from where there would be no second chance at escape. Hindy and the injured soldier were laughing again, but not Mrs Hindy, who was telling them to stop and trying to reach up, to help him, only to be met by Teleki's gaze, desperate and pitiless, as he placed his boot squarely in the middle of her upturned face and pushed off, feeling her nose crack under the sole. And then he was up the ladder, rung over rung, and out of the manhole and running, while they called after him to help pull them out.

Sándor stopped, intending to continue, but the audience had begun booing in Teleki's direction, the sound growing louder and louder until he left the stage.

Strangely, Teleki slept very well that night. There was something about surrender that was incredibly calming, as if the loss of desire could compensate for defeat. But by the middle of the next day he was squirming again, sitting in the cafe with his agent, who was showing him one article, feature and editorial after another, all of them reporting on the 'creative sabotage' of his lectures. In keeping with Teleki's recent luck, the writers devoted far more space to Sándor than to him, mainly because none of them had been able to dig up a single thing about this blind man tapping his way out of nowhere to deliver his long apocalyptic monologues, setting the record straight and exposing the liars. In these articles Sándor was a moral force and Teleki a con man.

'There's one here that speculates on whether you guys are working together,' said the agent, pushing across a copy of the *New York Times*.

Teleki glanced at it for a second and then quietly told his agent he was quitting.

'Quitting!' the agent responded. 'You can't quit!'

'I think I just need to disappear for a while,' said Teleki. 'Once this dies down we can talk about what to do next.'

'We? There is no *we*,' the agent told him. 'Not if you quit!'

Teleki looked at him, and in an instant realized what had happened. 'You've been talking to Sándor, haven't you? What, you're representing both of us?'

His agent looked out the window and then back at him. 'You know how often something like this comes around? A sleeper like this?'

'Tonight's my last show,' said Teleki, rising from the table.

It wasn't like Teleki to fulfil a contract – or any other kind of promise for that matter – if he didn't want to, and yet he found himself fighting the impulse to just walk away. Maybe he wanted to prove to Sándor that he wasn't afraid, that he couldn't be so easily chased away, that he could take whatever was thrown at him. But there was a more dangerous realization as well, and all that afternoon he seemed on the verge of confronting it, only to get scared and turn away, channelling what he felt into a rage so acute that more than once he was seen talking to himself, having imaginary arguments with Sándor from which he always emerged with the decisive victory.

By nightfall, though, shortly before he was due on stage, Teleki finally admitted to himself that Sándor's descriptions of the man using two children to get out of military service, or exposed by Pfeffer-Wildenbruch as a totally expendable soldier, or being mocked by Hindy and his men for cowardice was not without a certain comfort, as if there might be something to gain from having your stories turned inside out, from having the hard moral decision – whether to lie or tell the truth – taken away from you.

And when Teleki took the stage that night, standing on the podium, he was no longer the showman of six months ago, when Sándor had first turned up at his lectures, or even of the day before yesterday, when he'd tried to defend himself. There was something serious in him now, as if having come to the end of all this, having failed to defend himself, he was beyond loss, free, unconcerned for his reputation.

It was in his eyes, the need to survive, irrespective of honour or glory or anything else, as if he was once again looking at what Sándor had begun to describe, standing to interrupt Teleki five minutes into the lecture: the worst of what happened in the siege, all those men forced to take part in a breakout that should have happened months earlier and was now little more than a mass human sacrifice.

He remembered the morning, February 11, when a rumour went round that the radio operators had begun destroying their equipment; remembered the illusions many of the soldiers clung to: that only Romanians were guarding the breakout point; that they'd run the minute they saw the horde of fascist soldiers; that it would be no more than a half-hour march through the empty city to the place where German reinforcements were waiting; that, absurdly, the Russians were no match for the tactical brilliance of the Nazi and Arrow Cross commanders. Like Sándor, Teleki knew that Veresváry had assembled his men at the Bécsi Gate before the march, that they were hit by a bombardment out of nowhere, their bodies ripped open, dismembered, even before they'd had a chance to set out.

He could have followed Sándor word for word in recounting what only a very few men – a mere three per cent of the 28,000 who set out that day – could recount seeing, or refuse to recount, crushed as they were by recurring nightmares of that three kilometres of city, so overwhelming that to begin speaking of it would be to never speak of anything else again. Mortar fire along avenues and boulevards. Flares hanging in the sky overhead. Soldiers screaming in a rush of animal frenzy, all semblance of reason gone as they realized the Soviets were stationed along the route – that they'd prepared for the breakout, that tanks and rockets and snipers were in place to kill every single one of them – now crushed into doorways, stumbling in the dark, crawling over comrades missing arms and legs and begging to be shot – one last mercy for which no one could spare the time – pushed on by those behind them, a river of flesh squeezed out between the buildings bordering Széna and Széll Kálmán Square, into a night kaleidoscopic with shells, tracer bullets, flares, panzerfausts, the light at the end of machine guns flashing without pause, a city shattered into ever more impossible configurations – a maze without discernible routes, choices, even the certainty of dead ends.

There was a pause in the auditorium at the end of this. Then Sándor, gathering himself up, began to speak again, his glasses aimed at Teleki. 'This is what you saw when you emerged from the sewers. This is what you'd supported – you and the men like you – so eager to support Horthy when he signed with the Nazis, and then, when he was deposed for wanting to break with them, to shift that support to Hitler's puppet, Szálasi, and the Arrow Cross. *Honour!* you said. *Bravery! The nation above all!* But it was always someone else who paid for this allegiance, wasn't it? Not you. You slithered out of every situation, every duty you so loudly insisted upon, all those high standards and noble causes you so loudly proclaimed – always the job of someone else. And at the end of all that, in the aftermath, when you saw the breakout, realized what you'd done. . .'

'You went blind,' whispered Teleki into the microphone. 'You went blind.'

'I'm talking about you!'

'No you're not,' said Teleki, and he pushed back the lectern and walked off the raised platform and up the auditorium steps to where Sándor, who drew back as Teleki moved closer, was standing. 'This story you've been telling is your own, Sándor.'

'It's yours!' Sándor shouted. 'You know it's yours!'

And Teleki, in the most inspired performance of his career, threw his arms around the blind man, whispering, 'It's okay, it's okay, it's okay,' just loud enough to be picked up by the microphone pinned to his lapel.

He had tightened his hold until Sándor stopped struggling, and all the while he'd continued to whisper soothingly of how this was Sándor's public confession, how he could not have described the things he'd described unless he'd seen them, or known the things he knew unless he'd been there. He said he knew Sándor could still see, and that what had darkened his eyes was not physical in nature, but moral.

Sándor had shouted and hollered and tried to fight him off, but Teleki merely continued to hold him, and the audience had inclined their heads, finally, in sympathy, as if they'd never for a second thought of Sándor as anything other than a refugee from himself, using Teleki's lectures to disclose his conscience in the only way he could – obliquely, by projecting them on to someone else. They even clapped when Teleki finally let go of the exhausted, defeated Sándor and, taking him by the hand, led him from the hall, down the steps, out the back exit off the wings of the stage, where the blind man flung Teleki's hand away, told him he should be ashamed of himself, and stormed off as fast as the tentative tapping of his cane would allow, tripping over the first kerb he came to. Teleki smiled.

And he'd continued smiling late into the night, wrapped in his robe in the hotel, drinking the champagne his agent had sent up along with a note of apology Teleki never read, already knowing what it said. He gazed out over the city and wondered what Sándor might be doing now, whom he was with, where he was headed. For that was Sándor's way, Teleki had realized, incapable of functioning, of getting from one place to the next, unless there was someone, preferably a crowd, to help him, as if his blindness was a way of restoring people to some sense of community, as if by helping him they were ultimately helping themselves, as if there was another map of the world, not of nations and cities but of intersections of need, of what draws us together.

Sándor's world, Teleki thought. *His.* And he wondered for a moment what it was like – all those people working together – having long ago learned to count on nobody and nothing, groping his way all alone through the darkest of places. ■

CAPITAL GAINS

Rana Dasgupta

1

It all comes together on the roads.

Delhi is a segregated city; an impenetrable, wary city – a city with a fondness for barbed wire, armed guards and guest lists. Though its population now knocks up against 20 million, India's capital remains curiously faithful to the spirit of the British administrative enclave with which it began: Delhiites admire social rank, name-dropping and exclusive clubs, and they snub strangers who turn up without a proper introduction. The Delhi newspapers pay tribute every morning to the hairstyles and parties of its rich, and it is they, with their high-walled compounds and tinted car windows, who define the city's aspirations. Delhi's millionaires are squeamish about public places, and they don't like to go out unless there are sufficient valets and guards to make them feel at home, and prices exorbitant enough to keep undesirables out. But in this segregated city, everyone comes together on the roads. The subway network is still incomplete, there are few local trains (unlike Mumbai), and you can't take a helicopter to work (unlike São Paulo) – the draconian security regulations prevent that. So the Delhi roads accommodate every kind of citizen and offer a unique exhibition of the city's social relations.

On the eve of 'liberalization' in 1991 – when the then finance minister, Manmohan Singh, opened the economy up to global money flows, so bringing an end to four decades of centralized planning – there were three varieties of car on sale in India. The Hindustan Ambassador and Premier Padmini had both been around for thirty years and it took seven years to acquire one – production was limited to a few thousand a year and ownership restricted, in practice, to bureaucrats and senior businessmen. The compact Maruti 800, by contrast, was a recent arrival that had been conceived as a 'people's car': with a quota of 150,000 a year it had brought the possibility of private car travel within reach, for the first time, of the middle classes.

Nearly twenty years on, those three originals have all but vanished in the flurry of new brands that liberalization ushered in (though the stately Ambassador remains the preferred conveyance for Delhi's politicians and senior bureaucrats). The new economic regime stimulated more Indian companies, such as Tata, to start building cars, but it also brought in the global giants – Hyundai, then Ford, GM and Toyota, and sooner or later everyone else – and now, with car markets declining around the world, they are looking to India to take up some slack. India's car consumption is ten times what it was in 1991, and rising rapidly, and the effect in the cities is deadlock. The stricken carriageways are never adequate for the car mania, no matter how many new lanes and flyovers are built – and in Delhi, most cars are stationary much of the time. Hemmed in by the perpetual emergency of roadworks, and governed by traffic lights that can stay red for ten minutes, the situation is unpromising. Delhi drivers, moreover, never confident that any system will produce benefits for all, try to beat the traffic with an opportunistic hustle that often turns to a great honking blockage, smothered in the smoke of so many engines air-conditioning their passengers against the forty-degree heat. The main beneficiaries are foot-bound magazine sellers, who move fast and offer something to while away the time.

Another distraction for unmoving drivers: the endless automobile reveries posted up on hoardings – images of a parallel world where the roads are open, and driving is sexy and carefree.

With so many cars jammed up against each other, each as hobbled as the next, road travel could threaten to undermine the steep gradients of Delhi's social hierarchies. But here the recent car profusion steps in to solve the very problem it creates. The contemporary array of brands and models supplies a useful code of social status to offset the anonymity of driving, and the vertiginous altitude of Delhi's class system comes through admirably, even on the horizontal roads. Car brands regulate the relationships between drivers: impatient Mercedes flash Marutis to let them through the throng, and Marutis move aside. BMW limousines are so well insulated that passengers don't even hear the incessant horn with which chauffeurs disperse everything in their path. Canary-yellow Hummers lumber over the concrete barriers from the heaving jam into the empty bus lanes and accelerate illegally past the masses – and traffic police look away, for what cop is going to risk his life to challenge the entitlement of rich kids? Yes, the privileges of brand rank are enforced by violence if need be: a Hyundai driver gets out of his car to kick in the doors of a Maruti that kept him dawdling behind, while young men in a Mercedes chase after a Tata driver who dared abuse them out of the window, running him down and slapping him as if he were an insubordinate kid.

There is nothing superficial about brands in contemporary Delhi. This is a place where one's social significance is assumed to be nil unless there are tangible signs to the contrary, so the need for such signs is authentic and fierce. And in these times of stupefying upheaval, when all old meanings are under assault, it is corporate brands that seem to carry the most authority. Brands hold within them the impressive infinity of the new global market. They hold out the promise of dignity and distinction in a harsh city that constantly tries to withhold these things. They even offer clarity in intimate questions: 'He drives a Honda City,' a woman says, meaningfully, about a prospective son-in-law. Brands help to stave off the terror of senselessness, and the more you have, the better. Where the old socialist elite was frugal and unkempt, the new Delhi aristocracy is exuberantly consumerist. With big cars and designer accessories, it literally advertises its supremacy, creating waves of adoration and hatred on every side.

Somewhere around four a.m. on the morning of January 10, 1999 a car sped along Lodhi Road, a broad, leafy artery flanked by Delhi's parks and richest residential areas. At the wheel was a drunk young man named Sanjeev Nanda, who was returning home from a party with two friends. The car was a $160,000 BMW, one of the manufacturer's largest and most luxurious models, which had been privately imported and still carried foreign plates. Later estimates said it was travelling at 140 kilometres per hour; at any rate, it went out of control when it reached a police checkpoint and crashed through the barrier, ploughing into seven people and killing six instantly: three policemen and three labourers. Witnesses said that two men got out to see what had happened; when they saw the bodies and the screaming survivors, they got back in the car and drove off in a panic, running over one of the prostrate figures as they went.

Sanjeev Nanda was a charismatic twenty-one-year-old who had just graduated from Wharton Business School. His lineage was de luxe: his grandfather was Admiral S. M. Nanda, chief of India's Naval Staff, who, like several other well-connected figures in the Indian armed services, had made big money in his retirement by setting up as an arms dealer, brokering between foreign arms companies and his former colleagues. The business flourished further under the shrewd eye of Sanjeev's father, Suresh, whose acquisition of Delhi's elegant Claridges Hotel was only a small part of a network of investments and acquisitions he built in India and around the world.

After the accident, Sanjeev sped away to the nearby house of one of his companions, who were also from elite business families. This man's father owned a finance company and was used to grasping complex situations quickly: he immediately ordered his driver to move the BMW off the road and into his compound. The front of the car was covered in a gory mat of blood and flesh, and the guard was given the job of cleaning it up. But it had left a trail of leaking oil as it fled, which the police were able to follow to the house. They turned up in the middle of the clean-up, arrested Sanjeev and took him, still drunk, into custody.

The case should have been simple, but it melted away under the backstage influence of the Nanda family. Manoj Malik, the only one of the seven victims to survive his injuries, changed his story during the trial to say that it was probably a truck, and not a BMW, that hit him. The only independent witness, Sunil Kulkarni, who had been passing by that night and had described bodies flying over the BMW's roof, withdrew his testimony and said that he had made it under pressure from the Delhi Police, who were supposedly conspiring against Sanjeev Nanda. Sanjeev himself alleged he had not been in the car that night, which was registered in his sister's name, and denied any connection to the incident. The Nanda family tried to dissipate ill feeling by making unofficial payments to the victims' families. The case lost steam and life went on. Out on bail, Sanjeev did an MBA at INSEAD in Fontainebleau, near Paris, became managing director of the family hotel business, and moved into a penthouse at Claridges. Manoj Malik mysteriously disappeared.

Suresh Nanda's business was hit with unfortunate publicity: an undercover investigation into arms procurement corruption carried out by journalists from the news magazine *Tehelka* found that he had paid large bribes to government ministers in return for favourable consideration of his clients' products. He was charged with corruption and let out on bail while the Central Bureau of Investigation looked into his affairs. It emerged that he ran an Internet procurement monopoly that gave him a guaranteed cut of the vast business of government tenders, and the press expressed outrage that he could continue to enjoy this privilege even as that same government had him under investigation. Before long, he was caught offering a bribe of 100 million rupees ($2.1m) to a tax official who was offering to hush up the investigation, and he and Sanjeev, who was also involved, were sent to jail for fourteen days.

Then the BMW case took a new turn. The discredited witness, Sunil Kulkarni, in an attempt to show the world what pressure he was under, took undercover television journalists to a secret meeting with representatives of the Nanda family. This operation revealed that the Nandas were paying the lawyers on both sides of the case, who were working together to keep Kulkarni silent. The lawyers were dismissed and the case was finally heard in the Supreme Court. In September 2008, nine years after the incident, Sanjeev Nanda was convicted of mowing down six people while driving in a drunken condition, and sentenced to five years' imprisonment – an extraordinary moment when, contrary to expectations and experience, it was shown that the Indian elite cannot always make its acts disappear.

Contemporary Indian society is transfixed by wealth. A new genre of popular magazine is filled from cover to cover with features about gold-plated bathtubs, diamond-encrusted mobile phones and super-de luxe vacations, allowing readers to wallow in what they can never afford. Television game shows give weight to the seductive whispers of the market, showing working people in the very moment they are transformed into millionaires. People love to read about the possessions, opinions and talents of India's leading industrialists, some of whom have succeeded in creating quasi-religious cults around themselves. Criticism of the rich results in astonishing waves of rebuttal by ordinary people who feel it is an attack on their national pride.

But this determined adoration of the rich coexists with something else: something more crepuscular, full of fear and night-time jolts. In a society as stratified as this, it is possible to imagine that the ones at the top enjoy endless freedom – freedom so absolute that the only adequate use of it would be cruelty. For most people, Delhi life remains gruelling and deprived, the inconceivable promise of the global market unfulfilled, and this feeling of perpetual deficit lets in apprehensions of a vampiric ruling class, sucking the plenitude away from everyone else. This is the feeling that finds resonance in the story of Sanjeev Nanda, which has become one of Delhi's most popular parables. This story erupts into the public domain with the delicious nausea of something widely felt, but rarely observed: the recklessness of this economic system, its out-of-control heartlessness. Sanjeev's speeding BMW is a symbol of gleaming, maleficent capital, unchecked by conscience or by the roadblocks of the state. The scene of the impact, a one-hundred-metre stretch of road strewn with organs, severed limbs and pools of blood, is like a morality painting of the cataclysmic effects of this marauding elite in the world of ordinary people.

In this nightmare version of the rich, they are no longer the pride of the nation but invaders from outside, representatives of trans-national currents who are never authentically committed to the Indian good. Much was made, in the Sanjeev Nanda story, of his British passport and his imported car, as if his fatal velocity was that of foreign forces whose impact, here in India, could only be catastrophic. The Indian road has not been given over to speed as it has elsewhere; it is a place of innumerable modes of transport, a place of commerce, leisure and bureaucracy, a place cluttered with history. Even the most powerful men in the country cannot expect that clean lines will open up for them through the Indian reality. Only someone with no connection to that reality could imagine such a thing.

The society that has emerged in post-liberalization India is one consumed both by euphoria and dread. The rich are the emblems for both these sentiments, which is why they never settle into a single meaning. They are the simultaneous saints and demons of contemporary India, and any consideration of them oscillates with powerfully contradictory feeling.

2

In the Western press, the face of the 'new India' is typically urbane. It might be that of the exquisitely suited Azim Premji, chairman of Wipro Technologies, and staple of every Asian power list, who studied at Stanford, inherited a successful vegetable oil company and turned it into a global technology enterprise. It could be the face of Nandan Nilekani, co-founder of Infosys Technologies, *Forbes Asia*'s 'Business Leader of the Year 2006' and author of the recent *Imagining India: Ideas for the New Century*. English-speaking, intelligent and articulate, these billionaires are the kind of men the West can do business with. They are regularly invited to explain India's economic growth to international business conferences and journals, where they project a rational and understated image of the country. They reassure Western audiences that the 'new India' will be no more than an annexe of the old West: that the future of India, and therefore, to some extent, of the world, will be intelligible and familiar.

In truth, however, the anglicized class to which Azim Premji and Nandan Nilekani belong is becoming marginalized from Indian society. Immense upheavals are afoot, and English-speaking sophisticates now speak about themselves as harried and besieged. They still enjoy many privileges, but as time goes on they see their values and sensibilities disappearing from the media and the streets, and they are faced with the troubling realization that they no longer rule this society or dominate its imagination – or even understand the first thing about it.

Rajiv Desai, a fan of the Beatles and *The New Yorker*, who spent twenty years working in Chicago before returning to Delhi and setting up one of India's leading PR firms, is quite clear: 'Many of my friends are moving to Goa. There are so many people like me who have a second home in Goa, which is the only place you can still find anglicized values. People have intelligent conversation. There's standing room only in the jazz clubs. My house in Goa's not a country home, it's a *second home*, where I go to be myself and preserve my sanity. I can't stay the whole year in Delhi. It's backward. You take your life in your hands on the roads, you see the kind of people there are. It's been taken over by Hindi-speakers and loud Punjabi festivals like *Karwa Chauth* that no one used to make a fuss about twenty years back.'

The Indian economy of the turn of the twenty-first century has been far too explosive for the tiny English-speaking class to monopolize its rewards. In fact they have not even been its primary beneficiaries. Their foreign degrees and cosmopolitan behaviour prepare them well for jobs in international banks and management consultancies, where they earn good salaries and mix with people like themselves. But they are surrounded by very different people – private businessmen, entrepreneurs, real-estate agents, retailers and general wheeler-dealers – who are making far more money than they are, and wielding more political power. These people may come from smaller cities, they may be less worldly and they may speak only broken English. But they are skilled in the realm of opportunity and profit, and they are at home in the booming world of overlords, connections, bribes, political loopholes, sweeteners – and occasional violence – that sends their anglicized peers running for the nearest cappuccino. Over the last few years, provincials have become Delhi's dominant economic group, with many millionaires, and a few billionaires, among their number, and networks of political protection that make them immensely more influential than those who have become rich on a salary.

Saif Rizvi, a sociable young plastic surgeon who grew up mostly in Saudi Arabia and the United States, is one of many who are affronted by the new arrivals. Prominent Muslims from Lucknow, his family traces its lineage back 500 years, and Saif has a healthy contempt for Delhi's upstarts: 'Oh my God, the nouveaux riches. Yeah, I see them everywhere I go, man, you see the way they walk into the clubs, the way they order their drinks. They're horrible. The only thing those guys have that's nice is their cars. The nicest cars pull up and the most horrible people get out. Horrible bodies, horrible teeth, horrible voice modulation.'

Saif moved from New York to Delhi to take over the family clinic when his father was killed by a truck on a road in Uttar Pradesh two years ago, and he is gloomy about his new surroundings. He is alienated by Delhi conversation and he takes refuge in expat social evenings: 'I'm not impressed by Delhi since these guys came into money. Now the clubs cater to them, the TV and everything. Everywhere they play Bollywood music, man, that's what these guys like.'

A DJ in his spare time, Saif plays the sort of psychedelic trance that gives Delhi's Cambridge- and Berkeley-educated youth a good environment to take MDMA and escape from the city's grind. 'The Ministry of Sound set up a club in Delhi and you know what kind of music they played? Bollywood. Can you believe it? The Ministry of Sound is supposed to be cutting edge, and they play Bollywood songs! Just to keep those guys happy!'

Unfortunately for Saif, the laments of disdainful cosmopolites like him carry less weight these days. The city now looks to the Bollywood-loving provincials, who have reaped billions in the early twenty-first century boom, and turned the city's club-like mentality upside down. The rewards of that boom have flowed to them because its implausible escalations rode on the one thing they had that Delhi people did not: land.

In 1957 Prime Minister's Jawaharlal Nehru's government consolidated the capital's planning and development agencies into the new Delhi Development Authority. The DDA had sole responsibility for planning and executing the city's expansion and development and, in order to fulfil this, it had the right to acquire land forcibly and at greatly reduced prices. It was a development monopoly, whose exclusivity was guaranteed by laws making it impossible for private individuals or companies to own more than a few acres of land within Delhi's borders.

The DDA was given such enormous power over the landscape of this new capital that one can only be awed, today, by the mediocrity of its achievements. The drab, mouldering tower that the agency calls home is fully indicative of the DDA's preferred architectural style; the countless housing developments it has built across Delhi are warren-like and poky, and by now they are leaking and falling down. Nehru Place, the ugly office complex built by the DDA in the 1980s, is in ruins, and has now been mostly abandoned by companies fleeing to new accommodation outside Delhi. Nehru Stadium, which the DDA built for the Asian Games in 1982, has had to be entirely rebuilt in order to serve for the Commonwealth Games in 2010.

Such physical rot is an outward indication of the enormous corruption that gripped the DDA in its heyday of the 1970s and 1980s. Since no one else could own land for development, the agency was able to control the entire construction business – and to charge money for access. It would keep the supply of land low, sitting on its bank of rusty, disused plots and selling building contracts to the highest bidder. Building contractors would then claw the expense of their bribes back, once they were given a contract, by cutting every kind of corner on construction. In a city of Delhi's size and prestige, this racket was big business, and some of the largest fortunes in the city were made by mid-level DDA engineers whose job it was to rubber-stamp new projects – and many of them resisted promotion out of these lucrative positions for years.

But the disaster of the DDA created a set of other, unexpected effects, whose long-term impact was even more momentous. With the city of Delhi completely sealed to private commercial development, a number of individuals began in the 1980s to buy up land in the surrounding states. It was a quiet and laborious process, and most of the people who began it were not from the urban elite. They came from small towns, they understood how to do business with farmers, and they operated in areas that seemed impossibly backward and remote to Delhi businesspeople.

One of these men was Kushal Pal Singh, who came from a small town in Uttar Pradesh, and whose father-in-law's real-estate business was decimated when the DDA was set up. Singh was charged with reviving the business, later called DLF, and in 1979, unable to operate in Delhi, he began to buy up rural land to the south of the city, in the state of Haryana. This is how he describes the process:

I did everything it took to persuade these farmers to trust me. I spent weeks and months with their families. I wore kurtas, sat on charpoys, drank fly-infested milk from dirty glasses, attended weddings, visited the sick. To understand why this was important, it is necessary to understand the landholding pattern. The average plot size in Gurgaon [one of Haryana's nineteen districts] was four to five acres, mostly held by Hindu undivided families. Legally, to get clear titles, I needed the consent of every adult member of these families. That could be up to thirty people for one sale deed. Getting the married daughters to sign was often tricky because the male head of the family would refuse to share the proceeds of the sale with them. So I would travel to their homes and pay the daughters in secret. Remarkably, Gurgaon's farmers sold me land on credit. I would pay one farmer and promptly take the money back as a loan and use that to buy more land. The firm's goodwill made them willing to act as bankers for DLF. But it also meant I had to be extra careful about interest payments. Come rain or shine, the interest would be hand-delivered to each farmer on the third of every month at ten a.m. We bought 3,500 acres of land in Gurgaon, more than half of it on credit, without one litigation against DLF.

When men like Singh first called Delhi building companies to trudge out into the far-off brushland and build middle-class apartment complexes, the contractors thought they were mad. They drove out in jeeps, lurching over the baked earth, and stood in the naked expanse, where brightly turbaned villagers lived in huts and tended goats, and they wondered which Delhi banker or advertising executive would ever venture there. But by the 1990s, Delhi was caught in a real-estate crisis. Delhi's mega-city population was growing faster than anyone could build, and the city had little space left for new housing developments. The DDA had made almost no provision for commercial real estate, and big companies were operating out of cramped domestic basements. The quaint community markets built in the socialist era were entirely inadequate for exhibiting the products of the new consumer economy. So when Gurgaon opened its doors, proclaiming a 'new Singapore' of glass office blocks, gated communities, golf courses and shopping, it did not take long for the corporate classes to respond. Flush with boom cash, India's banks handed out loans to anyone who asked, and house prices were rising so fast that it made sense for everyone to put their savings into property. Microsoft and its ilk built their Indian headquarters in the thrilling emptiness of the Haryana countryside, and Gurgaon quickly became the largest private township in Asia, a dusty, booming expanse of hypertrophic apartment complexes, skyscrapers and malls. In 2007 Singh listed his company on the Indian stock exchanges; the 2008 *Forbes* list estimated him to be the world's eighth-richest man, with a fortune of 30 billion US dollars.

Gurgaon was only the largest and most prestigious of many such developments across Haryana and Uttar Pradesh, and Singh's fortune only the most fabulous of countless others. The land surrounding Delhi was an amazing commodity, doubling in value every three or four years, and multiplying its value sixty times with the simple addition of bricks, concrete and a bit of cheap labour. The new millennium saw a desperate land rush. Hundreds of thousands of acres of agricultural land were sold on to developers. Companies that had previously made their money from other things suddenly switched to real estate, and major banks and financial service firms such as Deutsche Bank and Morgan Stanley queued up to fund them. Small-time developers from drab little towns like Ghaziabad became serious property moguls who bought mansions in Delhi, threw glitzy parties with Bollywood star entertainment and sent their sons to US business schools to learn how to run billion-dollar businesses. Even farmers walked away from land deals with a few million dollars, and bought hulking SUVs for their sons, who brought them to Delhi and drove with macho glee around the seat of power. Such windfalls were often quickly spent, but the more astute of these families set up real-estate businesses, and took further slices of the pie. Some of the real-estate agents who had set out on their mopeds a few years ago to sell all this new property now received Mercedes and apartments as bonuses. As

A worker bends steel at a construction site in Gurgaon, a suburb of Delhi and a centre of India's new property boom

always, politicians made a killing. Prime Minister Nehru, for whom agriculture was sacrosanct, had cast stringent rules to prevent just such a land grab as this, and Uttar Pradesh's legendarily entrepreneurial politicians made sure that people paid well to have such an august tradition overturned.

This bonanza privileged those whose business methods were catholic. It was nearly impossible to operate at any significant scale without a wide network of paid connections among politicians, bureaucrats and the police. Moreover, amid such intense competition, the acquisition frenzy sometimes abandoned the delicacy of Singh's recollections. Real-estate mafias grabbed country houses in Haryana and employed senior policemen to silence the owners by filing false criminal charges against them. In Uttar Pradesh, they forced farmers and tribal communities to sell them their land under threat of violence, employed the local police to clear the residents off, and sold it on at a large profit. There was a general escalation of criminality and violence, and the people who came through with new fortunes were a formidable breed. They knew how to hijack state power for their own private profit, and they enjoyed the support of the police and of much-feared extortion gangs. Such people had cracked the muscular equation of contemporary India, and they spurned its liberal platitudes as just so much pious cant. These were the ones who became suddenly and gleefully conspicuous in Delhi, arousing the resentment of people like Rajiv Desai and Saif Rizvi.

During all this action in Haryana and Uttar Pradesh, Delhi's own property prices had reached fairy-tale levels. In 2006, at the height of the boom, industrialists and property moguls were paying almost 1.5 billion rupees (then 33 million dollars) for Delhi mansions. Even retired army officers or journalists, to whom the state had given spacious plots at knock-down prices in the 1950s, suddenly found they were sitting on property worth 2 or 3 million dollars – and since they often didn't have much in their bank accounts, they decided to sell. But like everyone else selling property in Delhi, they set the official price low and took the majority of the money in cash so as to reduce the tax bill on their profits. Who could buy property at those prices on those terms? What kinds of people were walking around with, say, a million dollars in cash? It was not the cosmopolitan children of the original Delhi middle class, who worked as PR executives or TV newscasters, and for whom a million dollars of black money was a tall order. These people were moving out of the city into Gurgaon flats. No, the people with the suitcases of cash were, as likely as not, property tycoons, industrialists, politicians or criminals. The capital of 'shining India' was being systematically handed over from its middle classes to a new black-money elite, and it was this group which was increasingly setting the tone – aesthetic, commercial and ethical – for everyone else.

3

Tarun Tejpal, editor of *Tehelka*, is a prominent Delhi figure who has devoted the last decade of his life to documenting corruption and violence in the twenty-first-century Indian ruling class. His magazine made its name with a sting operation in which senior government ministers were videotaped accepting bribes in return for their consideration of the products of a fictional British arms company, and boasting openly about other money they had made in this fashion. Another *Tehelka* sting operation helped to put the son of a powerful Haryana politician behind bars after he shot a waitress dead for refusing to serve him a drink: the gunman had been acquitted by the courts, but *Tehelka*'s intervention showed that the witnesses had been paid off by his family. *Tehelka* has published an unparalleled study of the 2002 slaughter of 2,000 Muslims in the state of Gujarat – a set of interviews that proved what many suspected: that the state had actively colluded in the event. The magazine has tirelessly documented the ongoing land grab by which vast tracts of Indian territory are seized from farmers and handed over to corporations under the recent Special Economic Zones Act. In a country of complacent, celebrity-happy newspapers, *Tehelka* is a major journalistic achievement, and one might expect Tarun to be quietly satisfied. But he is not.

'No one cares,' he says. 'There are no ideas except the idea of more wealth. The elite don't read. They know how to work the till, and that's it. There's nothing: we are living in the shallowest decade you can imagine. Rural India, that's 800 million people, has simply fallen out of the master narrative of this country. There should have been an enormous political left in India, but people worship the rich and there's no criticism of what they do. They face no consequences; they live in an atmosphere of endless possibility.'

'Do you think anything will come of all this money they're making?' I ask. 'Do you think they'll try to leave behind a legacy?'

'They don't care about their legacy! This is a Hindu society: I'm back for a million more lives – how much fuss am I going to make about this one? Indian businesspeople might run a school or feed a few orphans, but they're not interested in reform because they are bent on making the system work for them. Hinduism is very pliable. It rationalizes inequality: if that guy is poor it's because he deserves it from his previous lives, and it's not for me to sort out his accounts. Hinduism allows these guys to think that what they get is due to them, and they have absolutely no guilt about it.'

There's an incredible energy to Tarun. Messages arrive constantly on his two mobile phones, and he answers them without a break in his tirade. Over the course of the last few years, while managing a weekly magazine, he has somehow found enough spare time to write two novels. The second, *The Story of My Assassins*, has recently come out. It is a devastating portrait of Indian society, a tale of such hopeless horror and violence that the reader is left beaten down and without response.

Tarun is never lost for words, but as we talk I get the feeling that he too is becoming disillusioned. *Tehelka* has got him into a lot of trouble: he has faced death threats for his journalism, and ministers have tried to bury him with tax investigations and libel suits. The magazine runs on a shoestring: advertisers have stayed far away and corporate funders have been advised to pull out. Tarun is a well-connected man from a good army family, but over the last few years many of his connections have turned away. Some have even suggested that he is in the pay of foreign agents and that this is why he writes so critically of the Indian state. All this has left him wondering whether the enterprise of trying to tell the truth as he sees it – 'Free, fair, fearless' goes *Tehelka*'s slogan – is simply pointless.

'The dominant mood is frenzied accumulation,' he says. 'The corporations and the state are in bed with each other, eating and drinking the country out of everything it has. The Ganges is becoming a trickle: the most fertile river basin in the world. But the truth is that no one is interested in what's really going on. We don't even have a vocabulary to talk about it.'

To find a reason big enough for such a startling predicament, Tarun burrows into history.

'It all goes back to colonization: we're a damaged people. We were a subordinate race for three hundred years and it's made us envious. Now people are coming into wealth for the first time, they're discovering goodies, and they want them for themselves. They don't want anyone spoiling the party. Their parents were completely different: they weren't extravagant, they never ate out, they were still inspired by Gandhi. This generation has nothing in its head except goodies.'

Our conversation is brought to an end by the arrival of Tarun's next visitor. As I leave him I find myself looking for ways out of the sealed box of his hopelessness. I can't disagree with his morose assessment of what is happening around us: it is difficult to live here and not be stupefied by the speed and brutality with which every resource is being fenced in, mined and commodified. But is it true, as he implies, that north Indian Hindus are simply programmed by their history and religion to be rapacious? *Capitalism* is rapacious, and its new elites, wherever they have been in the world, have usually risen sternly. Is the new Indian elite worse than everyone else? Is it worse, moreover, than the socialist ruling class that went before? It is so common, these days, to hear people indicting the vulgar new India, as Tarun does, by comparing it unfavourably to the more genteel socialist system of the old days. But wasn't the socialist elite just as cruel and corrupt, even as it quoted Shakespeare and Marx? Isn't there much that is positive in the explosive dynamism of the contemporary Indian economy?

I go to have lunch with a psychotherapist, Anurag Mishra. I tell him about a man I recently met who told me a story curiously similar to the Sanjeev Nanda incident.

'His son called him to say he had just killed a man with his car,' I say. 'The son was in a panic and didn't know what to do. There were injured people lying on the street. The father told him, *Get out of there as quickly as you can.* His son had borrowed his car but he was only sixteen and shouldn't have been driving at all. So he told him to run. Isn't that surprising?'

'Not really. He's an Indian father, and he'll protect his son above everything else. A car accident is a matter of perception, it's a trick of fate, but a father's duty to his son is absolute. Do you think he's going to say, *Confess to what you have done and pay the price?* This isn't a guilt culture. In the Indian psyche, you dissociate yourself from the bad things you have done, and then they're not yours any more. That's why you can never make any accusation stick to a businessman or a politician. They won't even recognize the crimes you're accusing them of. They'll probably have you beaten up for insulting them.'

We are in an Italian-style cafe. Anurag is talking too much to touch his Caesar salad.

'Delhi is a city of traumas,' he says. 'You can't understand anything if you don't realize that everyone here is trying to forget the horrifying things that have happened in their families. Delhi was destroyed by the British in 1857. It was destroyed again by Partition in 1947. It was torn apart by the anti-Sikh rampages of 1984. Each of these moments destroyed the culture of the city, and that is the greatest trauma of all. Your entire web of meanings is tied up in culture, and if that is lost, your self is lost.'

He tells me stories of clients of his who have been torn apart by returning memories of Partition horrors – memories they had successfully buried for sixty years. He tells stories of the recollections of violence and deprivation that remain frighteningly persistent even in the minds of those who have made good money in the last few years.

'That's why Delhi is by far the most consumerist city in India,' he continues. 'People buy obscene amounts of stuff here. Delhi has an impoverished symbolic vocabulary: there hasn't been enough time since all these waves of destruction for its symbols to be restored. If I don't have adequate symbols of the self, I can't tell the difference between *me* and *mine*. So people buy stuff all the time to try and make up for the narcissistic wound. It's their defence against history.'

'Don't you think it will get boring after a while? If it's as you say, people will surely realize after a while that buying stuff isn't solving anything. Maybe they'll try something else? Maybe their children will rebel?'

Anurag smiles.

'This is very interesting,' he says. 'You know about the Oedipus complex? Freud said this was the universal condition of young men: they unconsciously want to kill their fathers and sleep with their mothers. That's the source of revolutionary energy – you kill your father symbolically by rejecting all his values and finding new ones. But I don't think this applies to Indian men. I would analyse Indian men in terms of what I call the Rama complex. In the epic poem *Ramayana*,

Rama gives up the throne that is rightfully his and submits himself to enormous suffering in order to conform to the will of his father. Indian men don't wish to *kill* their fathers, they wish to *become* them; they wish to empty themselves out of everything that has not come from their fathers.'

Like Tarun, Anurag sees the fundamental structures as fixed and preordained, even as the surface of Indian life changes so fast. Once again I struggle to find a way out. Surely it's not enough to say that the business elite is so in thrall to its own wounds and traumas that it cannot restrain its own reckless impulses, for these people are striking primarily for their astonishing boldness, not their limitations. I ask Anurag about his own relationship with money.

'During the British time,' he says, 'my grandfather was a freedom fighter. After independence he became a Congress politician. My father was a college teacher and member of the Communist Party. Both of them were idealistic and frugal, and I was always taught to think that people with money were bad. They had to be doing something seedy, and probably criminal. At school I envied the boys with money because they had stuff I wanted, but I also thought they must be bad.'

We've finished lunch by now and moved out to the cafe's terrace so that Anurag can smoke one of his beloved cigars.

'I didn't have money for most of my life and it was a big problem for me when I began to practise as a psychotherapist. I didn't know how to relate to myself as someone with money. I didn't really believe that I deserved money, or that I had the right to charge for my services. When I first got money I started eating a lot and I got very fat. I ate bad things, just wanting to fill myself up. I've only made my peace with money quite recently. I've lost all that weight. Now I think it's okay to give myself good things. Like this lunch. I don't have to have twenty bad things: I can have one good thing, and it's better than that excess.'

As he talks I realize how complicated it must be for him to watch the unrestrained consumption of the new rich with whom he shares his city. I realize that, for a certain segment of the anglicized middle

GRANTA

THE MAGAZINE OF NEW WRITING

Make a gift of good writing with a Granta subscription – fiction, reportage, memoir, biography and photography five times a year

Buy a twelve-month subscription for a friend and receive, with our compliments, a *Granta* special-edition **MOLESKINE**® notebook

Subscribe online at **www.granta.com** or call **toll-free 1-866-438-6150** or fill in the **back of this card** and send to us

'Provides enough to satisfy the most rabid appetite for good writing and hard thinking'
WASHINGTON POST BOOK WORLD

Gift subscription offer: take out an annual subscription as a gift and you will also receive a complimentary *Granta* special-edition **MOLESKINE®** notebook

GIFT SUBSCRIPTION 1

Address:

FIRST NAME: LAST NAME:

ADDRESS:

CITY: STATE:

COUNTRY: ZIP CODE:

TELEPHONE:

EMAIL:

GIFT SUBSCRIPTION 2

Address:

FIRST NAME: LAST NAME:

ADDRESS:

CITY: STATE:

COUNTRY: ZIP CODE:

TELEPHONE:

EMAIL:

YOUR ADDRESS FOR BILLING

FIRST NAME: LAST NAME:

ADDRESS: CITY:

STATE: COUNTRY: ZIP CODE:

TELEPHONE: EMAIL:

NUMBER OF SUBSCRIPTIONS	DELIVERY REGION	PRICE	SAVINGS	
☐	USA	$45.99	32%	All prices include delivery
☐	Canada	$57.99	32%	YOUR TWELVE-MONTH
☐	Rest of World	$65.99	32%	SUBSCRIPTION WILL INCLUDE FIVE ISSUES

I would like these subscriptions to start from:

☐ the current issue   ☐ the next issue

PAYMENT DETAILS

☐ I enclose a check payable to 'Granta' for $_____ for _____ subscriptions to *Granta*

☐ Please charge my ☐ MASTERCARD ☐ VISA ☐ AMEX for $_____ for _____ subscriptions

NUMBER ☐☐☐☐ ☐☐☐☐ ☐☐☐☐ ☐☐☐☐   SECURITY CODE ☐☐☐

EXPIRATION ☐☐ / ☐☐   SIGNED   DATE

☐ Please check this box if you would like to receive special offers from *Granta*
☐ Please check this box if you would like to receive offers from organizations selected by *Granta*

Please return this form to: Granta Subscriptions, PO Box 359, Congers, NY 10920-0359, Call toll-free 1-866-438-6150 or go to **www.granta.com**
Please quote the following promotion code when ordering online: **BUS107PMG**

class, the new rich offend sentiments that are so deep and complex that the only possible response is profound anxiety and revulsion. I realize that there really is no simple way out of the gloom they feel about the present moment; I understand why these conversations always hit dead ends.

If people like Tarun and Anurag refer back so nostalgically to the socialist period it's because, no matter how hypocritical it was, the socialist regime at least took the trouble to legitimize itself in terms they could recognize. This modicum of intellectual correspondence with the ruling class seems positively alluring now that the people who are shaping their world are so adamantly opaque. Where possible, the new Indian elite runs private companies that have no shareholders and no scrutiny – and often it conducts its ground-level operations through a myriad of other companies whose ownership is deliberately obscure. It amasses invisible fortunes and pays very little tax. It does not like to seek funds from public sources; instead it forms alliances with other secretive and cash-rich elites, such as the Russian billionaires. It keeps such a low profile that some of its richest and most enterprising individuals have no entries on Google. It operates behind high walls; it is energized, rather than outraged, by the immense disparities in the world, and it is pretty much indifferent to public outcry or media exposé: you can think whatever you like, there is no dialogue.

I can find little reassurance for someone like Tarun Tejpal. There is nothing trivial about his feelings of outrage and impotence. They are feelings, in fact, that accompany the north Indian business class wherever they go: both Mumbai and Bangalore have significant political movements devoted to protecting local society against the ferocious business acumen of north Indian entrepreneurs. It is true what he says: in these times it is difficult to make any mark on Indian public life through the subtlety or distinction of one's thought. People whose talents and tastes lie in that direction can do what they like; for the time being the rules are set by others.

And perhaps Tarun's are the dominant global feelings, in fact, of the times to come – for the new Indian elite is charismatic and muscular and ultimately well reared for the age of globalization. In all their grandiose unsentimentality they remind us that a lot of the comfortable myths we have been told about capitalism are simply that. In truth, it is a flailing, terrifying thing.

4

Monty Chadha makes a timid entrance into the quiet hotel lounge where he has asked me to meet him. He wears a black turban and suit; he is stocky and muscular and speaks with a faint lisp. He is twenty-eight years old.

He is not particularly talkative. I try to break the ice by telling him that we have a friend in common and we talk about her for a while. He relaxes. I ask him about his life.

'Until I was a teenager,' he says, 'I thought my dad worked for the government. I used to ask, *Why do we have this big house?* They told me, *Your grandfather built it, then we lost the money and now your dad works for the government.*'

In truth, Monty's father ran a large assembly of businesses across the states of Uttar Pradesh, Haryana and Punjab. The mainstay of this empire was liquor retail, a business which, in gangster states like Uttar Pradesh, offers rewards only to the shrewd, charismatic and violent. Other people with Monty's background have told me how they grew up hearing their fathers giving assassination orders over the phone – but at this early point in the conversation Monty is too professional to share such details.

'Of course there were goons around – you can't run this kind of business without a strong arm – but my dad always kept them out of our sight. He believed in discipline. He said, *If you do bad things, like if you get caught for drunk driving, I can't get you off.* A lot of powerful people said to their sons, *I can get you off anything.* It makes for a different kind of mentality. Of course, later I discovered that there was nothing I could have done that my dad couldn't have got me off.'

Monty's father is present throughout his conversation as a kind of spiritual touchstone.

'The company was set up by my great-grandfather in 1952. When my father took it over in the 1980s the family was in debt. Now the group has an annual turnover of 1 billion dollars. My father's will to succeed is phenomenal. If he sets out to do something, he will get it done. If there's someone I want to become, it's him.'

Monty speaks about the family business in the first-person plural. He has grown up absorbing business ideas and techniques, and they are a natural part of his speech.

'When our liquor business was at its height we controlled nineteen per cent of Indian liquor retail. At that time, the government auctioned liquor outlets to the highest bidder. Later on it introduced a lottery system to prevent monopolies. But we could still grow the business because we had so many employees. In any lottery in our region, out of one hundred entrants, eighty were our men.'

Monty was sent to a series of expensive schools, but he was repeatedly expelled, and at the age of sixteen he dropped out for good. He went to London for a year or two to have fun: clubs, parties and everything else that a teenager with a well-stocked bank account can think of.

When he came back he was put in charge of one of the family's sugar mills. But his heart was not really in it – and the real-estate boom was on. In 2001 the family set up a real-estate business and Monty, twenty-one and entirely untrained, was given the task of building the largest shopping mall in northern India.

'When I was in England I spent a lot of time walking around malls, studying how they were made. There's no point reinventing the wheel. I know more than anyone in India about how you set up a mall, how you arrange your brands. My father had no experience in a professional context, so everything I know about the professional context I've learned myself. I introduced computer systems into the business. I taught myself Oracle programming because the professional contractors were no good. Then I taught myself all about the latest building techniques. Centrestage Mall was built with special prefabricated steel pillars, which had never been used in Indian malls before. Recently, I taught myself finance. I read finance texts online and every time I didn't know a word I looked it up. Six months ago I didn't know anything and now I can conduct finance meetings with Pricewaterhouse.'

Centrestage was famous for having Delhi's most luxurious, high-tech nightclub, Elevate. It was Monty's pet project, his personal party zone, with endless champagne for him and his friends – and his nightly arrival there, surrounded by bodyguards, always provided a frisson.

'For a time I was *the man* in Delhi. Loads of people wanted to be my friend. Women wanted to sleep with me. I said to my wife: *if I hadn't been married, things would have been very different.* A lot of people were very fake.'

Like many Delhi rich boys, Monty was given a big wedding as a way of winding down his wild years. When he was twenty-two, he married his childhood sweetheart, Shanam Kochar; their reception had 6,000 guests and featured dance routines by Bollywood stars Diya Mirza and Shilpa Shetty. Monty still loves parties, and, as I discover during our conversation, he becomes relaxed and witty with alcohol, but there is no doubt that he has by now grown into a fully fledged partner to his father. He's ready to shut down Elevate: he doesn't have time to attend to it any more, and he doesn't want anyone else to run it. He operates five shopping malls across India, and he has another 1,400 acres under development. And that is just the beginning. He is moving on to much bigger plans.

'We've just leased 700,000 acres for seventy-five years; we're opening up food processing, sugar and flower plantations.'

He is so matter of fact that I'm not sure if I've heard correctly. We have already discussed how laborious it is to acquire land in India, buying from farmers at five or ten acres a time. I can't imagine where he could get hold of land on that scale.

'Where?' I ask.

'Ethiopia. My father has a friend who bought land from the Ethiopian president for a cattle ranch there. The President told him he had other land for sale. My dad said, *This is it, this is what we've been looking for, let's go for it.* We're going in there with [exiled Russian oligarch] Boris Berezovsky. Africa is amazing. That's where it's at. You're talking about numbers that can't even fit into your mind yet. Reliance, Tata, all the big Indian corporations are setting up there, but we're still ahead of the curve. I'm going to run this thing myself for the next eight years, that's what I've decided. I'm not giving this to any CEO until it meets my vision. It's going to be amazing. You should see this land: lush, green. Black soil, rivers.'

Monty tells me how he has one hundred farmers from Punjab ready with their passports to set off for Ethiopia as soon as all the papers are signed.

'Africans can't do this work. Punjabi farmers are good because they're used to farming big plots. They're not scared of farming 5,000 acres. Meanwhile, I'll go there and set up polytechnics to train the Africans so when the sugar mills start up they'll be ready.'

Shipping farmers from Punjab to work on African plantations is a plan of imperial proportions. And there's something imperial about the way he says *Africans.* I'm stunned. I tell him so.

'Thank you,' he says.

'What is on that land right now?' I ask, already knowing that his response, too, will be imperial.

'Nothing.'

Monty is excited to be talking about this. His spirits seem to be entirely unaffected by the recession that currently dominates the headlines. He orders another beer, though we have exceeded the time he allotted me. All of a sudden, I find him immensely charismatic. I can see why he makes things happen: he has made me believe, as he must have made others believe, that he can do anything. I ask him how he learned to think like this.

'I'm only twenty-eight,' he says. 'Why not?'

He becomes flamboyant.

'We're going to be among the top five food processors in the world. You know the first company I'm going to buy? Heinz.'

I'm interested in his *Why not?* Is it on the strength of such a throwaway reason that nearly three-quarters of a million acres of Ethiopia are being cleared and hundreds of farmers shipped across the world? I wonder what the emotional register of this is for him. It seems as if, somewhere, it's all a bit of a lark.

'I sometimes wonder why I work,' he says. 'I do ask that question. I don't need to work. But what else am I going to do? You can't sit in beach resorts for three sixty-five days a year. So I think of crazy things. I like it when you think up something and it's so wild you're messed in the head and you think, *How can I do this?* – and then you think, *Why not?*'

I feel like pointing out that life holds more possibilities for someone like him than just sitting on the beach. *Messed in the head* sounds like language that remains from his wild days, as if the whole thing is about getting a high. I ask him how he wants to spend his money.

'Currently I drive a BMW 750i. It's good for long drives to the mall I'm building in Ludhiana. The car I really want is an Aston Martin DBS. But I'll buy it later, when I deserve it more. My father wanted to buy me a nice sports car three years ago but I said, *Wait.* I set myself certain goals. By the time I'm forty I want a 160-foot boat. I want a nice Gulfstream plane. And I want to be able to run them without it pinching me.'

Monty talks as if he were saving up for a motorbike or a fridge, and suddenly he seems strangely banal. This is a man who can dream up earth-bending forms of money-making, but his ideas of spending it are consumerist in the most ordinary of ways. His middle-class vocabulary seems at odds with his multi-billion-dollar international economy, and I wonder if he is deferring his sports car so as not to run out of future acquisitions too quickly. I wonder if the whole enterprise does not teeter on the edge of senselessness, if he is not in fact still waiting for someone to supply him with a meaning for this money around which his life is organized.

Unprompted, he becomes philosophical.

'I'm not religious. I'm spiritual. My basic principle is whatever goes around comes around. It will come back to you, you can be dead sure of that. I live my life in a Vedic way. Disciplined. No idol worship, no stupid acceptance. Also that you don't just let someone hit you and take it from them. You give it back to them.'

I'm not sure if this last point flows from the basic principle, but I don't question it. Monty is deadly serious. He is letting me in on his knowledge. He tells me a story.

'I was at a party recently and the waiter was handing out drinks and he moved the tray away a little too soon and this guy hadn't got his drink. So the guy shook up a soda bottle and sprayed it in the waiter's face. I went straight to the host and I had him chucked out of the party. You have to know how to behave. Some people only feel they have money when they can screw someone else, and then they feel, *Okay, I have money.* You have to know how to treat normal people. You see, there are two kinds of rich. There are people who've had money for a long time and they don't give a fuck who you are. They'll be nice to you anyway. Like I'm nice to people. You may get bored being around them, because all they talk about is how they've just got back from Cannes or St-Tropez, but they won't kick you out. But the people who've got rich in the last five years, they turn up at a party and the first thing they do is put their car keys down on the table to show they have a Bentley. They don't know how to behave.'

Monty is a little drunk, and he's policing boundaries that are clearer to him than to me. It's not the first time he's said that people have to know how to behave. Once again I feel that his stand against the nihilism of the Delhi rich is all the more fervent because he is assailed by it himself. He is intimate with all the thuggish bad boys who have given people like him such a bad name ('It's so sad what happened to Sanjeev Nanda,' he says, 'he's such a sweet guy') and he is impressed by parables of restraint.

'I have a friend who's a multibillionaire,' he says, 'and I asked him about the best car to buy for your kids, because I've just had kids, and he suggested a Toyota Innova. He could afford to buy a jet for his kids but he doesn't. They have to earn it. He just buys them an Innova. You see, people say there are bad kids but it's all the parents' fault. It's totally the parents. They have fucked up their kids and once that's happened it can never be undone. One day the guy is driving a Maruti 800, the next day he's driving an S Class, and he buys Beamers for his kids when they're ten years old and they just go crazy. The kids get fucked up.'

I've had a number of conversations with people in Monty's economic class and they all talk about Delhi as a kind of El Dorado, where fortunes pour in overnight, almost without your asking. *In this country, at this time,* they say, *you've got to be an absolute fool to go wrong.* But for all the talk of 'new money', most Delhi fortunes are not, strictly speaking, new. They have certainly exploded in the last few years, and small-town powerhouses have indeed turned into metropolitan, and even global, ones. But they rest on influence, assets and connections built over many decades, and in that sense they are wholly traditional. The sudden prominence of a new, provincial elite should not lead one to think that the economy has become somehow democratic. People like Monty have always had money, and they see the world from that perspective. The gruelling, arid Delhi of so many people's experience is not a city they know.

'Where do you place yourself in the pyramid of Delhi wealth?' I ask. 'There can't be many people turning over a billion dollars?'

'You have no idea,' he says, and smiles condescendingly.

'This year's *Forbes* list counted about twenty billionaires in this country. How many do you think there really are? At least a hundred. Most people don't go public with their money. They don't want scrutiny. I would never list my company.'

'Who's the most powerful person in Delhi?'

'It all depends on politics. You can have a billion but if you have no connections it doesn't mean anything. My family has been building connections for two generations and we know everyone. We know people in every political party; we never suffer when the government changes.'

'So why do you travel with bodyguards?'

'The UP police intercepted communications about a plan to

kidnap me, and they told my father. People want money and they think of the easiest way, which is to take it from someone who has it. They can't do anything constructive themselves so they think short term. We need more professionalism in India. More corporate governance. Then we'll show the entire world.'

For good reason, Monty is grateful to India.

'Since I was fourteen I've realized India is the place. I love this place, this is where it's at. Elsewhere you may have as much money as Laxmi Mittal but you're still a second-class citizen. This is your fucking country. You should do it here.'

Monty tells me how he hates America.

'Why should Wal-Mart come in here? I don't mind Gucci and Louis Vuitton – they do nothing to disturb the social fabric. But keep Wal-Mart out of here. We were under slavery for seven hundred fucking years. We've only been free for sixty. Give us another thirty and we will buy Wal-Mart. I tell you, I was at a party the other day and I had my arms round two white people and I suddenly pushed them away and said, *Why are you here? We don't need you guys any more.*'

Twenty-eight years old, well travelled and richer than most people on the planet, Monty's resentment towards white people is unexpectedly intense. I ask him how the world would be different if it were run by Indians.

'It will be more spiritual,' he says. But then he thinks for a moment and says, 'No. It will be exactly the same.'

I bring our conversation to an end. Monty pays the bill and we walk outside to the quiet car park.

'Thanks,' he says, shaking my hand. I don't really know why.

His driver opens the back door of his BMW and Monty gets in. The gates open, the BMW sweeps out, and behind it an SUV full of bodyguards.

Monty lives about 200 metres away.

I drive home, thinking over our conversation. I ponder a little detail: during my loo break he took advantage of my absence to send a text message to our common friend. Just checking that I really knew her.

Somewhere in Monty is something alert and intimidating.

I'm still driving when he sends a text message to me, asking me not to quote certain things he has said. I write back: OK IF YOU ANSWER ONE MORE QUESTION. WHAT DOES MONEY MEAN TO YOU?

He responds straight away: ONE OF THE END PRODUCTS OF MY HARD WORK, IT DOES MEAN A LOT I RESPECT IT IT GIVES ME MORE HARD WORK AND ON THE SIDE A BIT OF LUXURY (:

5

Driving past Delhi's sole dealer of Bentleys and Lamborghinis, I stop in on a whim and ask to speak to the manager. He's not around and I'm sent to have coffee with the PR girls. They are appropriately attractive and, judging by their diamonds, from the right kinds of families ('I've driven a million Porsches and Ferraris,' says one. 'They're nice cars. But when you get into a Lamborghini it's something else'). For them, Delhi is a place of infinite money-making and they fall over themselves trying to express this fantastic fecundity.

'When someone comes in here looking to buy a Bentley, we don't ask him what he's driving now. Just because he drives a BMW doesn't mean he can afford a Bentley. We ask if he has a jet or a yacht. We ask if he has an island.'

'Are there many people with jets in Delhi?' I ask.

The girls wax apoplectic.

'*Everyone* has one. And not just one – they have two, three, four.'

We chat about nice cars and expensive living. A Lamborghini is driven into the showroom: the noise is so deafening that we have to stop talking until it's in place. I ask the philistine's question: what's the point of spending 30 million rupees ($635,000) on a car that can do over 300 kilometres per hour in a city where the traffic doesn't move? They tell me about the car club that meets at night in the diplomatic enclave, where the roads are straight, wide and empty.

'You have to have at least, like, a BMW or a Mercedes to join. They meet at midnight and they race their cars. The Prime Minister's office is always calling us to complain.'

'Why?'

'Because the Prime Minister can't sleep. These engines make so much noise they keep him awake. So he calls us to complain, but obviously there's nothing we can do.'

As I drive away, I cannot help thinking of Prime Minister Manmohan Singh tossing and turning in bed, his snowy hair unturbaned on the pillow, his dreams interrupted by the rich boys' Ferraris screaming up and down the roads outside. Manmohan Singh is of course the man who, long ago, as finance minister, opened up the economy and set the course for a new market elite. ∎

From the Journals of Mahmoud Darwish
1941–2008

Translated by Catherine Cobham

As if he were asleep

He woke up all at once. He opened the window on to a faint light, a clear sky and a refreshing breeze. He felt his body, limb by limb, and found it was intact. He looked at the pillow and saw that no hairs had fallen out in the night. He looked at the sheet and saw no blood. He switched on the radio and there were no reports of new killings in Iraq or Gaza or Afghanistan. He thought he was asleep. He rubbed his eyes in the mirror and recognized his face easily. He shouted: 'I'm alive.' He went into the kitchen to prepare coffee. He put a spoonful of honey in a glass of fat-free milk. On the balcony he saw a visiting canary perched on a tub of flowers he'd forgotten to water. He said good morning to the canary and scattered some breadcrumbs for it. The canary flew away and alighted on the branch of a bush and began to sing. Again, he thought he must be asleep. He looked in the mirror once more and said: 'That's me.' He listened to the latest news report. No new killings anywhere. He was delighted by this peculiar morning. His delight led him to the writing desk, with one line in his head: 'I'm alive even though I feel no pain.' He was filled with a passionate desire to make poetry, because of a crystal clarity that had descended upon him from some distant place: from the place where he was now! When he sat at the writing desk he found the line 'I'm alive even though I feel no pain,' written on a blank sheet of paper. This time he didn't just think he was asleep. He was sure of it.

A gun and a shroud

'Nobody will ever defeat me, or be defeated by me,' said the masked security man, charged with some obscure task. He fired into the air and said: 'Only the bullet should know who my enemy is.' The air responded with a similar bullet. The unemployed passers-by weren't interested in what went on in the mind of a masked security man, out of work like them, but he was seeking his own private war since he hadn't found a peace to defend. He looked at the sky and it was high and clear. As he didn't like poetry he couldn't see the sky as a mirror of the sea. He was hungry, and his hunger increased when he smelled falafel, and he felt his gun despised him. He fired up at the sky in case a bunch of grapes might fall on him from paradise. He was answered by a bullet, which kindled his suppressed enthusiasm for a fight. He rushed forth into an imaginary war and said: 'At last I've found work. This is war.' He fired on another masked security man, hit his imaginary enemy and received a trifling wound to his leg. When he returned home to the camp, leaning on his rifle, he found the house crowded with mourners and smiled because he thought they thought he had been martyred. He said: 'I'm not dead!' When they informed him that he had killed his brother, he looked contemptuously at his gun and said: 'I'm going to sell it to buy a shroud worthy of my brother.'

REALITY, REALITY

Jackie Kay

N*ow that – that is bursting with flavour. I'm getting ginger, and then I'm getting lime coming in at the end there. That is a sensation. That is delicious. I could eat up the whole plate.* Today I told myself I was going to have a positive day. Today was day one of *My Big Week*. I got up early and scrubbed the face with cold water. I was shallow of breath due to the excitement. I couldn't stop talking to myself. I couldn't quieten down. Here's the voice, going duh duh duh duh duhhh non-stop. *Can you win? Have you got what it takes? Are you going to shoot yourself in the foot? Get egg on your face? Hmmmm? Only the extremely talented survive. It's all about separating the wheat from the chaff. Only the ones with that special extra ingredient, delicate as sorrel, mysterious as saffron, wise as sage, magic as a glittering sheet of gelatine, only the crème de la crème rise to the surface!* COOKING *doesn't* GET *tougher* THAN *this*! I was shouting now into the mirror. Big voice! Big flavours! I rinsed my face enthusiastically again and again and again. I dabbed my face dry and confessed soberly to my dark-eyed reflection: *we're looking for elegance.*

But truth be told, I was feeling a bit ropy on account of drinking too much whisky the night before. I've been drinking whisky because it's good exercise for my palate. Me drinking a different whisky is like an artist trying a new colour. It's part of my culinary training, sniffing and detecting. This one was a top dram – 73.32 – and, just to perfect my expertise, I sniffed several times and swirled before saying to myself: 'Stef, what can you smell?' I was watching *24* and I turned it down because they were putting me off my stride. I can smell polished wood, polished wood and maybe pear drops. Suddenly, there was Ali and I sharing sweets in the park with the burn near the house I grew up in. I had pear drops and she had Italian creams, which only our Italian cafe seemed to do, exquisite sweets – a kind of fudge with a thick, dark chocolate bottom – and we both had shining eyes, girls' eyes, excited to be in each other's company. Maybe that's it; it's downhill all the way from then. There's nothing like the old excitement of girls. Where did they go, the old pals of the babbling brook? I was swirling the whisky and getting a kind of crème brûlée flavour sneaked in at the end, or maybe vanilla custard. I had three doubles to be sure. Yep. Orange peels and vanilla custard. Then I staggered up the steep stairs to bed and the whisky roared me to sleep. It wasn't a lullaby. It was loud, a sailor singing *speed bonny boat* at the top of his voice. Finally, I think I landed up on Skye and fell asleep remembering the time when I went to the south of Skye on holiday, a cottage near the Aird of Sleat, and I met a man who said, 'Have you been to the north of the island?' I said, 'Yes,' and he said, 'I dinna like it up there, it's much too commercialized.' And he was talking about three shops! Or the time when I was in a pub in Orkney and England was playing Germany and England was winning four to one, would you believe, and a wee man's voice shouted out, 'C'mon Germany!' and everyone laughed. I went to sleep thinking about that, and thinking about my big day. I said, 'C'mon Stef! You've some day ahead. Get yourself some shut-eye, do yourself a favour.'

★

Well, so here we are on the first day of *My Big Week*, and I'm absolutely determined to excel. But first things first! Feed the dog breakfast! I haven't yet stretched to gourmet meals for my mutt, so I get out a tin and open it, absolutely no point sniffing the tin for notes of offal. It's an awful smell, dog food. I take the dog round the block. Can't wait to get back to my kitchen! I've got a stopwatch, a set of kitchen scales, a new KitchenAid, a heavy-bottomed pot, a sharp knife, a good chopping board. Cost me a wee fortune, but money well spent. It cost much less than the five-day trip to Florence I'd been thinking about, or the seven days to Lake Garda. I reckon I'm bang on the money: *holiday at home is the new going away*. I've taken a week off work. Well, I'm sick paying a single supplement to go on holiday on my own. I mean what nonsense! Hello? Pay extra for a single bed? Huh? What kind of person thought that up? Did they sit down one afternoon with a cup of tea and think to themselves, Aha! Let the recently bereaved, the dumped, the chucked and the lonely pay more, they're a waste of space? Don't get me started! One of the reasons I'm putting myself through the HEATS is to see if the HEATS might control my RANTS and stop me veering off the subject. Focus, *Chef Stef*, this is what is asked of you today. Extreme focus; absolute commitment. You've got twenty minutes. There is absolutely no room for error. *Let's Cook!* – the voice of the greasy-haired one. I'm good at doing his voice. I frighten myself with my own brilliant mimicry! Talk about intimidating. *Let's Cook!*

Timer set for twenty minutes, no cheating. Twenty minutes exactly. Was tempted to give myself twenty-three, but what's the point in cheating on myself? It's like pretending to the weighing scales you've lost more than you've lost. The scales know and so do you. I crack three eggs on the dot of twenty and swiftly whisk them. (I might develop upper-arm muscles as a side benefit.) I chop mushrooms, parsley and red onion. I roast a red pepper. (The greasy haired one, again!) I grate some Gruyère cheese and slice some soda bread. *Ten minutes!* I cook the mushrooms and the parsley and the red onion together. *Five minutes!* I grill the tomatoes. I skin and then slice the red pepper. They are all ready! I slip the eggs into the pan and cook on a medium to hot heat, then I add the separate ingredients and fold over. *Thirty seconds! Plate up!* I stand back from my plate, quickly, sneakily, sprinkling parsley over the omelette as my timer rings. *Stand back from your bench! Time's up!* I was out of breath. *OhMyGod*, it all mattered *so much!*

I sit down at my table, ten thirty a.m., a little later than planned, to eat the first HEAT meal of the day. I'd made a fresh pot of Earl Grey tea, fresh leaves, note, not tea bags, sniff, and some soda bread toast. I don't have time to look at the morning newspaper and see what's going on in the world. I'm sweating, anxious about what was going to be said. *You've played it safe with an omelette,* the fat-faced friendly one says. *To be honest, I'm a little disappointed. And what a lot of work you gave yourself. Nice, but not very inspiring. Where's the flamboyancy in an omelette? Ah but what an omelette,* the greasy-haired one says. *This must be the best omelette I have ever eaten in my entire life!* As he enthuses, I realize that it's his approval I want most of all. *I'm getting the Gruyère flavour, that lovely warm roasted red pepper.* I suddenly sink and flag, the air going out of me like an imperfect soufflé. I'm depressed with my lack of ambition. An omelette! Call yourself a chef, Stef, and that's what you produce for the semi-finals? You better smarten up girl, or you're going home. *The Girl needs to push herself. The Girl needs to raise her game.* I need to get to the shops, pronto, for lunch's and dinner's ingredients. Some holiday this is turning out to be! Walkies, I say to my dog who is the only one who seems to listen to me these days. She wags her tail and sits by the front door while I double-check things. Now, now, Stef, think positive, you can still turn yourself around. There's still time for self-improvement. I try to walk fast, but I can't walk fast because I'm carrying fifteen stone, which since I tried my new 'Whisky Diet' is a lot less than I was a few weeks ago, when I was sixteen and a half stone, before I was promoted to the semi-finals. Low carbs – that's the secret. That's why the whisky is a necessity. No carbohydrates in whisky. Little-known fact, that. People out there don't know the difference between carbs and calories, but don't get me started.

I walk into my local fish shop, Out of the Blue. I know they know I live alone. If you buy one tuna steak on a Wednesday and one red mullet on a Thursday and splash out and buy one piece of sushi and one piece of halibut on a Saturday, there's no hiding the absolute extent of your aloneness. Sometimes the man throws in tails of organically smoked haddock out of sympathy. Once he gave me a free free-range chicken which had lost both its hind legs, but other than that was in pretty good nick. I couldn't tell if it lost its legs while still alive or not. Don't let's go there. I buy a piece of halibut and a hake steak in Out of the Blue; some fresh spinach, rocket, pear and hazelnuts in the Unicorn; a small piece of Gorgonzola in the Barbican. It seems silly facing the long queue and taking my number, number thirty-four, for four ounces of Gorgonzola but I am emphatic about sticking to my chosen ingredients. A lot of people veer dramatically away from the shopping list; not me.

I take my dog through the Beech Road park and on the way back I bump into another dog owner, who is in quite a state. I don't know her name but I know her dog's. She says, 'I can't remember when I last got Gatsby wormed. I'm not sure if it's April she's due or now. If it's April I'd rather wait, last year I kept a diary. A dog diary!' – she laughs at herself like she is some kind of genius – 'But I forgot, and chucked it out, not thinking I'd need to check the dates for this year.' She throws her eyes up in the air like she is tossing a ball for her dog to fetch, and then she walks off. I am getting used to my only real intimacy coming from the confessions of dog walkers. It's amazing the things people tell me. A man stopped to chat the other day, a complete stranger with a Great Dane. He pointed to the slobbering, big-eyed dog and said, 'She gets jealous if I get a new woman. She's driven all the girls out, even the missus. She's the missus now, eh, eh?' I couldn't tell if he was proud or defeated. He rolled his eyes then he hurried off through the woods that lead you to the River Mersey which stretches all the way from here to Liverpool.

Today, I've really not got time to stand about chatting to dog owners. 'I'm up against the clock,' I say and hurry past the woman who usually stops while out walking her Scottish terrier and her Zimmer.

'Okay,' she says, her hands resting on the Zimmer. 'Nice day today!' 'Lovely, yes,' I say. 'Doing anything nice?' she says. 'I'm cooking cordon bleu! I'm in the semi-finals!' I tell her. She's the first person I've told. 'It's costing me more than the vet, all the expensive ingredients, but worth it!' 'Mmmm,' she says and looks a bit envious, or is it dubious, I'm not sure. I bid her farewell. For all I know the heights of her culinary expectations are a tin of Heinz Tomato Soup, followed by a tin of Ambrosia Creamed Rice.

Stop it Chef Stef! You've turned into a *well big snob* since you were picked for the semi-finals! I hope you're not going to leave your old friends behind? Of course not! I hurry through the small park with my Tibetan terrier following behind me. The tender yellow and purple crocuses are out and the modest white snowdrops. My dog stops to sniff the crocuses, pisses, then sniffs again (her equivalent to Chanel N° 5). The shy spring is here. What a relief! The trees are still bare but the leaves will be coming. I hope the schnauzer we often bump into is not coming out today. Damn. My dog stops for a poo now and I get out my plastic bag. I stop for a second while it cools; it's the warmth that bothers me most. When I pick it up, I try and think of what the consistency is most like – bread dough maybe, anyone? Clootie dumpling in the pillow? – and in this way I'm always thinking culinary thoughts even when performing a most unpleasant task. This, as it were, allows me to work on the job! I dispose of the plastic bag in the red dog bin. But the smell, I can't really stretch to comparing the smell to anything. Put it this way, it's not exactly fragrant. That's enough Stef; let your dog have her modesty. My dog is a bit embarrassed that I have to pick up her doo-doo, because she's a pernickety wee thing. If she were to hear my inside thoughts, she'd be mortified.

I arrive back home. Nearly time to start the timer and the lunch. It is one o'clock. No time for the lunchtime news. I am the news. I am the rolling news. I have lost a stone and a half and have started my own HEATS. I could perfect my style and earn a fortune. What would I call it? *The Whisky Diet?* (That would attract the fat alkies!) *You Diet and Dog Diets Too?* (That would lure obese people who uncannily resemble their obese canines.) For lunch, I'm serving a watercress soup to start followed by a lovely piece of halibut with a Welsh rarebit topping and a spinach, pine nut and raisin salad. I'm using up the Gruyère from the morning omelette. I ask myself: what are we looking for today from you Stef, do you think? A beautiful plate of food, I answer myself. I need to cook my heart out today. Need to take risks! It is do or die today. *Let's Cook!* I'm not hungry actually, but I must stick to the gruelling schedule, or I can't call myself anything.

I mix a tablespoon of Dijon mustard, two tablespoons of double cream and a cup of grated Gruyère into a paste, spread it on my halibut and put the halibut in the oven at 200 degrees. I set my timer for twenty minutes. A voice is screaming in my head. DO NOT OVERCOOK FISH! Meanwhile I wilt my spinach leaves but forget to squeeze out the excess water. OH NO! Then I toast the pine nuts, but burn them a little. HELP! Then I soak the raisins but soak them for too long until they look like the wrinkled eyes of very small, very old animals, beavers maybe, or badgers. I taste my watercress soup having whizzed it through the new KitchenAid that I bought specially for this special week, and cheap at the price too in a way – less than a week in the Costa Brava, or nine nights in Morocco, which would have been nice since I love Moroccan food. No, here was me, bravely à la Costa o Solo Mio, and soon, when I am truly brilliant, I certainly will be inviting people CHEZ *moi* and certainly will stun them with my big bold flavours and elegant presentation. *Stand back from your bench! That watercress soup is so green,* the greasy-haired one says. *That is delicious,* the fat-faced friendly one says. *That green reminds you of allotments, childhood, it's as fresh as spring. I'm getting that good iron. I mean, Phwoar! Phwoar!* I nod and look sage and try to hide my superior smile. I imagine the faces of the other contestants turning an envious green. *Now for the main. Presentation could be better. That spinach is looking a bit sloppy and has left a trail of water on the plate. You've let yourself down! Flavour good. Could do with more seasoning. I'm getting the sweetness of the raisins, but those pine nuts are burnt. This fish, nice idea with the Welsh rarebit topping, but a bit of a waste of a lovely fish, halibut.*

I don't agree with you, I say quietly. *At this level, you need to be better. You are going home, Stef. Sorry. You're going home.* You don't know what you're talking about, I say again. You're just a jumped-up pair of idiots. You wouldn't know a good meal if it slapped you in the face. You don't even like good food. Is it because I didn't do snail porridge? Too right I'm a bad loser! I feel myself being frogmarched round the kitchen. Someone shouts, *Cut! Take her off set!* I can hardly breathe. Some holiday this is for me. The stress! The tension! I've failed. I haven't made the final. I haven't realized my dream. I'm gutted like all the fish I've cooked. Devastated. The once in a lifetime opportunity has slipped through my fishing net. I see myself in the sad green room, not the dream room. I'm frank with the camera. There's no way I'm stopping cooking, I say to the little light in my kitchen that is really the eye of the burglar alarm but could just as easily be the eye of the watching world. No way. I've got my dreams. I could still turn up trumps and deliver the goods. Then they'd be the ones with egg on their face, ketchup on their pants – tossers. Complete and utter tossers. It's always the men they pick. How come the men get to be chefs and the women get to be cooks? It's a disgrace.

I take out my fine bottle of whisky. Make that a double. I've just narrowly missed the finals, whatdya expect? I was *that* close. Give me a break. Is this you drowning your sorrows, Chef Stef? Too right it is. Get it down! Pear drops? Teardrops, more like. Crème brûlée? Cry baby. I look at myself in the bathroom mirror. My face looks like a summer pudding. I've got myself all upset. A voice whispers, *You've one more chance. It doesn't involve anyone but you. Let's Cook. Come on, now, love.* It's a gentle voice, lovely, not my own. I think it sounds like the voice of my dead mother, but I can't be sure because I've forgotten her voice. I wish I could remember her voice exactly. What was it like? Like fresh spring water babbling down the Fintry Hills.

It is four hours and three minutes since I last cooked, and five hours and ten minutes since I last walked the dog, and one hour and six minutes since I last had a snooze and now it is time to prove myself.

My eyelids are swollen from crying, like little slugs. My face is all blotchy. But it's not about looks, being a chef, only your food needs to look beautiful really. I get out my blue-and-white striped apron that I bought specially, but had forgotten buying. Silly me! I tie a knot, confidently. Lucky apron. For starters: pear fried in ground coriander with hazelnuts, rocket and Gorgonzola salad with a sherry dressing. For main: hake steak baked with an onion and lemon-rind confit, new potatoes with mint, green beans with tomatoes, garlic and basil. To finish: a chocolate soufflé with raspberries on the side, a shortbread biscuit, followed by a small whisky. Make that a double. Make it 73.32, The Scotch Malt Whisky Society. Even though I don't live in Scotland any more, I wouldn't drink anything but Scottish whisky. Good malt is allowed for dessert. I say so, and it's my rules. This is me here doing this right now. I'm methodical. I tidy as I go along. They'd be proud, but the hell with them. My presentation is a sensation – back of the net! – and the idiots have missed it. Their loss! Everything is delicious. That is one plate of food. *That is one plate of food. That fish is cooked to perfection. Perfect. Lovely, elegant dish. Well done! Phwoar! That is outstanding! The Girl can cook. Well done.* I put the silver fish skin in the bin and start on the chocolate soufflé, rich, velvety, darkly enigmatic chocolate soufflé, tart serious raspberries. *Charming, absolutely delightful.* I knock back the whisky. *That is one cheeky wee whisky, inspired, absolutely, inspired and inspiring. Now that, that is almost alchemy! I mean like, wow!*

This is my reality: I'm losing weight, and it's a consolation. Bye-bye junk food, cheerio Big Mac! So long French Fries. It is falling off me. I don't need to lie to the scales any more. I can sing to the scales instead. But something's missing. I'm not a complete success story. Maybe because the dog's diet has been a disaster and the dog is still fat? Or maybe it'd be nice to have someone to cook for. My old friend Ali, what would she like to eat now? Maybe she'd prefer fish and chips to red mullet with lemon and bay? Maybe she'd love sea bream stuffed with fennel? I'm not sure. We were nineteen before we saw a corn on the cob. I was twenty-two before I tasted avocado. Didn't think much of it in the beginning, but that was because I tried to eat the skin as well. Then I had a terrible time with an artichoke, not a Jerusalem artichoke but the kind that has a heart. I ate the heart but I ate the hair round the heart too, and coughed for a week. The first meal I made was chilli con carne. I crunched into a whole dry chilli. The roaring inferno of pain in my mouth! It was agony!

Maybe I could cook Ali my special Arabic chicken with pine nuts and saffron, with a lemon pilaf and a green salad? I'd make sure I didn't burn the pine nuts this time. What else? I can't think. I can't think of anything. I'm tired out thinking about what to eat. It's exhausting. What a holiday! I'd have been better off trailing around the Vatican. At least I might have got to see the Pope.

It is the end of my week, and I've faced the biggest challenge of my life so far. I've got through a week completely on my own and next Monday I must go back to work and face the music. I don't really like my work colleagues. They moan all the time and they are intensely competitive. It is a whole culture of moaning. Anyway very soon, holiday over, back to face the music. Do you know where that expression comes from? Someone sits and stares at the radio; someone else won't take their eyes off the hi-fi; someone fixates on their piano until, what, until the music starts, and it lifts you, and lifts you some more, until finally you are not in your life at all, you're in another life entirely. That's what's going to happen to me when I face the music. It's going to be so different, so very, very fine. That is really going to happen to me. I'm like, can't wait. ■

AMERICAN POWER

Mitch Epstein

In Cheshire, Ohio, I watched backhoes crush whole houses into kindling in less than an hour. The destruction was so fast and easy, I had to remind myself these were real homes, not a child's cardboard constructions. At the local pizza shop, I photographed a newspaper that pictured a white clapboard house next to a power plant; across the roof in black marker, the shop owner had written GONE.

It was the fall of 2003 and I had been hired to photograph a town in the process of being erased. American Electric Power had paid residents of Cheshire a lump sum to leave, never come back and never complain to the media or in court if they became sick from environmental contaminates spewed out of the plant. The company was buying itself a lawsuit-free future. Back in New York, I could not get Cheshire out of my mind.

It was my visit to Beulah Hern that had made the deepest impression on me. 'Boots', as she called herself, was in her eighties and refused to sell her home. American Electric Power, she explained, was harassing her for being a hold-out, so she had taken her security in hand. Boots showed me two surveillance cameras installed at her window under a ruffled curtain. On top of her wooden television cabinet sat a video monitor. This enabled her to watch her favourite TV programmes and simultaneously monitor her backyard for suspicious activity. Here I was in the home of a genteel elderly woman who could have been my grandmother, except that this grandma had taken extreme measures to protect herself. Her security set-up unnerved me. It mirrored the coal plant's security. Surveillance was everywhere in the tiny town of Cheshire. Boots sat down in her easy chair and watched me as I photographed her video cameras. 'Would you like to see my gun?' she said, and from the side pouch of the chair, where I expected to find copies of *Reader's Digest* and the *Farmers'Almanac*, Boots pulled out a handgun. Sensing my alarm, she kindly unloaded it.

Six months later, in the spring of 2004, I began to make pictures of the production and consumption of energy in the United States. I wanted to photograph the relationship between American society and the American landscape, and energy was the linchpin; this much I had gleaned from Cheshire. Energy – how it was made, how it got used, and the ramifications of both – would therefore be my focus. For the next five years, I travelled the country making photographs at or near energy production sites: coal, oil, natural gas, nuclear, hydroelectric, fuel-cell, wind and solar. It was a strange kind of tourism: energy tourism. Everything I photographed related to energy, even if the link was not always obvious or simple. The electric chair in the West Virginia State Penitentiary in Moundsville, for instance, might appear incongruous. Yet, aside from being an icon of electrical power usage, the chair presses the question: for what exactly are we importing all of this oil, burning all of this dirty coal, and drilling into our oceans and our open spaces?

In my studio hung a giant map of the United States stuck with colour-coded pushpins: red for coal, blue for nuclear, green for wind, yellow for 'been there', and so on. My studio manager Ryan and I would plot my next trip while staring at the map. Before I could leave, dozens of queries went out to corporate public relations, plant managers, government bureaus, people living off the grid or stewing up biodiesel, congressional aides and cheap motels. The point of all that careful planning, though, was to set myself up for the unexpected. Having a clear plan was a ruse to launch me into the world and into the work. Much of the time, my favourite pictures were the result of serendipity.

Hurricane Katrina threw a painfully resonant wrench into my well-laid plans. I had already plotted a trip to Louisiana to photograph the offshore oil platforms and refineries along the Gulf Coast when the hurricane hit. Six weeks after the initial devastation, I went to see the rigs and what remained of the coastline. Even before this disaster, scientists had connected the dots between energy production, climate change and an increase in deadly weather. Katrina was the ultimate emblem of how we, as a society, had failed; how our rapacious, 'supersize-me' culture had led to this catastrophe. The oil platform I photographed on Dauphin Island, Alabama was an unmoored mangle of bent and broken steel. It brought to mind a great prehistoric creature that has finally been crushed by something greater.

I travelled many times to photograph the repercussions of westward expansionism on the landscape. Mountains, rivers and deserts there supported dams, power plants, highways, oil wells and the occasional solar or wind farm. Humankind's technical prowess had etched itself into nature's grandeur. But early settlers did not expect that their American Dream of material ease would ultimately require more energy than the land alone could give. The Hoover Dam, for instance, a supreme feat of hydro-engineering in the 1930s, has now become an emblem of nature's depletion. In my photograph of the dam, it is hard not to be impressed by society's taming of the untameable: the harnessing of water to foster the growth of the American West. Pride is evident in the dam's magnificent architecture. But this image of human triumph also shows Lake Mead's diminishing waterline, known as 'the bathtub ring'. The ring is a result of a ten-year drought, as well as the siphoning off of water to nearby Las Vegas for luxury hotels and golf courses. Water itself has become more valuable than the electricity it can produce.

The wounds I discovered in the American landscape made me reconsider my own sense of entitlement and the American heritage of manifest destiny. These pictures question the human conquest of nature at any cost. Might we, as Americans, consider our obligation to nature and one another, not only our individual rights?

One right to which I cling, however, is the right to photograph in public space. Security and surveillance continually interfered with this right, and inadvertently influenced my pictures. There was a new sense of vulnerability in the United States after September 11, 2001 and I expected to be questioned now and then. But I resented the systematic harassment by police and guards that I faced while I worked on these photographs. Law enforcement officials more than once ran me out of town when I had done nothing remotely criminal. The result was that from 2003 to 2008 – a span that coincided, not uncoincidentally, with the Bush presidency – almost wherever I went to work in the United States, I went in fear. This was because my intentions ran counter to corporate interests, which had Homeland Security to back them up. I wanted to make the topic of energy more transparent, whereas big energy companies and their governmental counterparts shrouded themselves in secrecy.

The height of my security troubles came in the fall of 2004 when I returned to the Ohio River Valley. In Raymond City, West Virginia – more hamlet than city – a stranger proudly invited me into her backyard to, as she put it, 'appreciate a better view of the cooling towers'. A bench sat on the riverbank facing the Amos coal power plant. I imagined warm summer evenings when residents would drink a cold beer there and enjoy the view of the massive stacks as they belched toxic emissions into the sky above the Kanawha River.

In neighbouring Poca, I set up my camera on a public sidewalk and twenty minutes later the flashing lights of a four-wheel-drive police cruiser came towards me. A sheriff stepped out and shouted orders at my assistant and me. As she ran a check on our drivers' licences, another four-wheeler pulled up. Another sheriff got out and asked to search my car: 'You don't have a dead body in there, do you?' I handed him my rental keys and watched him rummage through our belongings, nervous that he might light-strike a sheet of exposed film. He returned with a stack of four-by-five, black-and-white Polaroids as evidence against me. The deputy and State Police had to be called now, he said, because I'd been photographing the power plant without authorization. I wanted to point out to him that I had been standing on public property, that I had been at a great distance from the plant, and that I also photographed an empty chair on the river's edge. But this was one of those times when you know that any comment you offer – however sensible – will make a bad situation worse.

Thirty minutes later, an unmarked car arrived. A middle-aged man in a suit and tie stepped out and flashed his ID: FBI. 'You know,' he said, 'if you were Muslim, you'd be cuffed and taken in for questioning.' Another unmarked vehicle pulled up, making the final count six vehicles and six law-enforcement officers. Passers-by must have thought there'd been a murder.

I was becoming less sure that this would end with a laugh and an apology on their part. Six officers huddled to discuss my fate. Five minutes later, the FBI agent returned to scold me. 'You can't just go pointing your camera at these infrastructures any more. Times are changing. Why didn't you tell me that you've been questioned for this kind of thing before?'

It was true – I had already gone through many interrogations by then. One resulted from a call the police had received in Shippingport, Pennsylvania, reporting a man on Main Street carrying a missile launcher. The missile launcher was my tripod. A police officer escorted me out of town, explaining that the power company I was photographing didn't allow pictures. I had broken no law, however, having attempted to photograph a coal stack from a public street in the centre of town. Apparently, Shippingport police now enforced corporate instead of constitutional law. I was witnessing the Patriot Act in action.

On a later trip to West Virginia, a public relations officer at the John E. Amos Plant welcomed me warmly and allowed me to make pictures inside the facility. I was shocked. It turned out he was a photography buff and had a copy of one of my books. His cooperation was an exception. The cops and FBI let me go after the nearly two-hour interrogation in Poca, but henceforth I worked with a discomforting urgency, sensing Big Brother at my heels. At one point, I consulted my attorney, hoping I could find a legal argument to use against the next officers who would lawlessly eject me. 'Don't get arrested at all costs,' he counselled, less than reassuringly. 'You don't want to end up in some small-town jail that won't be easy to get out of.'

Energy's symbiosis with politics was a given, so it made sense to visit the nation's capital. Ironically, I photographed a nuclear warhead at the Department of Energy (DOE) headquarters and a solar array at the Pentagon. Energy production is now a major concern of American military command, which is sponsoring several progressive renewable energy projects. I had expected an alternative energy display in the lobby of the DOE, which is, after all, charged with overseeing domestic energy production, research and conservation. Instead, the DOE displayed a nuclear missile – a vestige of the Department's predecessor, the Atomic Energy Commission, which began in 1946 to grapple with the dangers of the recently developed nuclear bomb. I couldn't help thinking it was time to change the display.

With energy politics in mind, I also went to both political conventions in the late summer of 2008. The Republicans were holding theirs at the Xcel Energy Center, Saint Paul, Minnesota; the Democrats were boasting a 'green' event in Denver, Colorado, sponsored by the so-called clean-coal industry. I nosed around the prison-like metal fencing that surrounded the hall in Denver, but never gained access. Neither did I get into the Xcel Center in Saint Paul. I had tried hard for each, and with good connections. But I was not a photojournalist who would promote the events in the news, which made me unnecessary and a potential liability. By this time, I was used to getting rejected from official venues. This project was, in part, about not getting in. What I saw on the outside, though, was less predictable and more intriguing to me than the choreographed hoopla inside the halls. I made a picture of the Fox News electronic billboard outside the Xcel Center, which showed the approach of Hurricane Gustav. Gustav halted the RNC proceedings for a day and brought back horrible and, for many politicians, embarrassing memories of their response to Katrina.

Between Denver and Saint Paul, I photographed the energy landscape of the Midwest. I visited a strip mine in the Powder River Basin of northeastern Wyoming, where the coal's purported cleanliness eluded my camera, which I had to wipe laboriously to remove the soot after the shoot. Three months later, in amazement, I watched a Christmas time television ad run by the coal industry, in which several chunks of coal with blinking eyes cheerily sang:

> *Frosty the Coalman is a jolly happy soul,*
> *He's abundant here in America and he helps our economy roll.*
> *Frosty the Coalman's getting cleaner every day,*
> *He's affordable and adorable and helps workers keep their pay.*
> *There must have been some magic in clean coal technology,*
> *For when they looked for pollutants there were nearly none*
> *to see…*

Should we believe this ad made by an industry that stands to make billions if we do? Or should we listen to Nobel Prize-winning energy expert Al Gore, who says clean coal is 'imaginary'.

Some bold steps are being taken towards a different energy future, but over ninety per cent of America's energy production and consumption remains non-renewable. In one of the strangest, most optimistic pictures I made, a young inventor named Chester Lowrey spun blue-white threads of electricity as vivid as Zeus's thunderbolt from a Tesla coil. The coil itself, invented in 1891 by Nikola Tesla, is a source of cheap, high-voltage ignition. It is no answer to our energy dilemma, to be sure, but one of Lowrey's experiments may eventually lead to one. This electrical DJ embodies, for me, the grass roots ingenuity that has historically improved American lives.

About a year into making this series of pictures, I realized that power was like a Russian nesting doll. Each time I opened one kind of power, I found another kind inside. When I opened electrical power, I discovered political power; when I opened political power, I discovered corporate power; within corporate was consumer, within consumer was civic, within civic was religious, and so on – one type of power enabling the next. I began making these pictures with the idea that an artist lives outside the nesting doll, and simply opens and examines it. But now – while America teeters between collapse and transformation – I see it differently: artists sit outside, but also within, exerting their own power.

When I photograph, I do not consciously think about politics. But it was inevitable that the grim reality of American power circa 2003–2008 would find its way into my work. I could not ignore the security excesses, corporate avarice and environmental indifference I encountered. I have tried to convey in these pictures not a political message, but the beauty and terror of early twenty-first-century America as it clings to past comforts and gropes for a more sensible future. ∎

AMERICAN POWER: PHOTOGRAPHS
Mitch Epstein

2.

3.

4.

6.

9.

10.

12.

13.

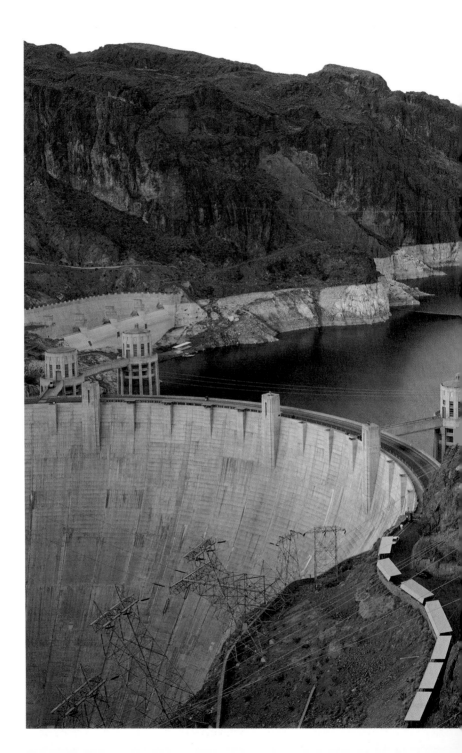

Picture titles

1. BP Carson Refinery, California 2007

2. Gavin Coal Power Plant, Burke County, Georgia 2006

3. Poca High School and Amos Coal Power Plant, West Virginia 2004

4. Wyodak Coal Mine, Wyoming 2008

5. Altamont Pass Wind Farm, California 2005

6. Amos Coal Power Plant, Raymond City, West Virginia 2004

7. Ocean Warwick Oil Platform, Dauphine Island, Alabama 2005

8. Martha Murphy and Charlie Biggs, Pass Christian, Mississippi 2005

9. Superdome, New Orleans, Louisiana 2005

10. Las Vegas, Nevada 2007

11. Iowa 80 Truckstop, Walcott, Iowa 2008

12. Altamont Pass Wind Farm, California II, 2007

13. Cheshire, Ohio 2004

14. Midland, Texas 2005

15. Hoover Dam and Lake Mead, Nevada 2007

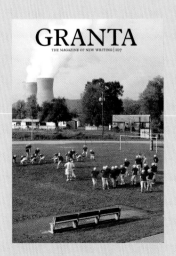

Yes, I would like to take out an annual subscription to *Granta* and receive a complimentary *Granta* special-edition MOLESKINE® notebook

PERSONAL SUBSCRIPTION

Your address:

FIRST NAME: LAST NAME:

COMPANY: ADDRESS:

CITY: STATE: ZIP CODE:

COUNTRY: TELEPHONE: EMAIL:

GIFT SUBSCRIPTION

Gift address:

FIRST NAME: LAST NAME:

COMPANY: ADDRESS:

CITY: STATE: ZIP CODE:

COUNTRY: TELEPHONE: EMAIL:

Billing address:

FIRST NAME: LAST NAME:

COMPANY: ADDRESS:

CITY: STATE: ZIP CODE:

COUNTRY: TELEPHONE: EMAIL:

NUMBER OF SUBSCRIPTIONS	DELIVERY REGION	PRICE	SAVINGS	
	USA	$45.99	32%	All prices include delivery
	Canada	$57.99	32%	YOUR TWELVE-MONTH SUBSCRIPTION
	Rest of World	$65.99	32%	WILL INCLUDE FIVE ISSUES

I would like my subscription to start from:

[ ] the current issue   [ ] the next issue

PAYMENT DETAILS

[ ] I enclose a check payable to '*Granta*' for $_____ for ____ subscriptions to *Granta*

[ ] Please charge my [ ] MASTERCARD [ ] VISA [ ] AMEX for $_____ for ____ subscriptions

NUMBER [ ][ ][ ][ ] [ ][ ][ ][ ] [ ][ ][ ][ ] [ ][ ][ ][ ]   EXPIRATION [ ][ ] / [ ][ ]

SIGNED _____   DATE _____

[ ] Charge my card automatically annually

[ ] Please tick this box if you would like to receive special offers from *Granta*

[ ] Please tick this box if you would like to receive offers from organizations selected by *Granta*

Please return this form to: **Granta Subscriptions, PO Box 359, Congers, NY 10920-0359, Call toll-free 1-866-438-6150** or go to **www.granta.com**

Please quote the following promotion code when ordering online: **BUS107PM**

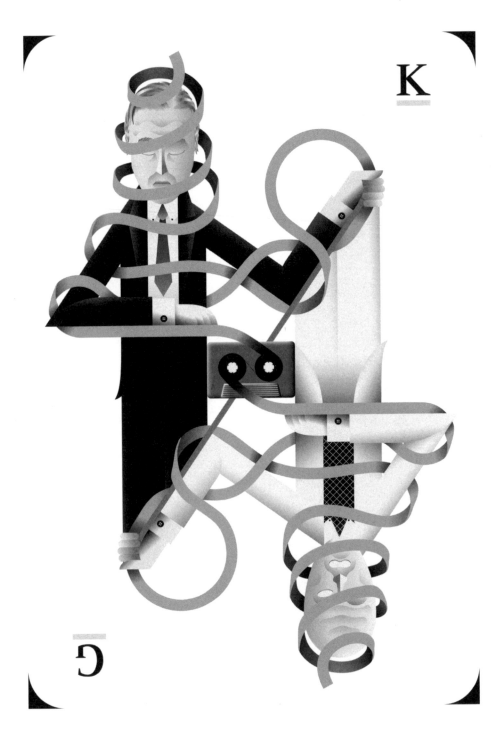

THE RULE OF TAGAME

Kenzaburō Ōe

Translated by Deborah Boliver Boehm

ILLUSTRATION BY EMMANUEL ROMEUF

1

K ogito was lying on the narrow army cot in his study, his ears enveloped in giant headphones, listening intently. The voice on the tape had just said, 'So anyway, that's it for today – I'm going to head over to the Other Side now,' when Kogito heard a loud thud. There was silence for a moment, then Goro's voice continued: 'But don't worry, I'm not going to stop communicating with you. That's why I made a special point of setting up this system with Tagame and the tapes. Well, I know it's probably getting late on *your* side. Goodnight!'

The recording ended on this rather vague and unsatisfactory note, and Kogito felt a sudden, excruciating sadness that seemed to rip him apart from his ears to the very depths of his eyes. After lying in that shattered state for a while, he put Tagame back on the nearest bookshelf and tried to go to sleep. Thanks in part to the soporific cold medicine he'd taken earlier, he fell into a shallow doze, but then a slight noise wakened him and he saw his wife's face glimmering palely under the fluorescent lights of the study's slanted ceiling.

'Goro committed suicide,' she said softly. 'I wanted to go out without waking you, but I was worried that Akari would be frightened by the rush of phone calls from the media.'

That was how Chikashi broke the news about what had happened to her only brother, Goro, who had been Kogito's close friend since high school. For a few moments Kogito just lay there in disbelieving shock – waiting, irrationally, for Tagame to start slowly vibrating, like a mobile phone receiving an incoming call.

'The police have asked Umeko to identify the body, and I'm going to keep her company,' Chikashi added, her voice full of barely controlled emotion.

'I'll go along with you till you meet up with Goro's family, and then I'll come back here alone and deal with the telephone,' Kogito said, feeling as if he were paralysed from head to foot. The avalanche of media calls probably wouldn't begin for a few hours at least.

Chikashi continued to stand silently beneath the fluorescent lights. She watched attentively as Kogito got out of bed and slowly put on the woollen shirt and corduroy trousers that were draped over a chair. (It was the dead of winter.)

After Kogito had finished pulling a heavy sweater over his head he said, 'Well, then,' and without thinking he reached out and grabbed Tagame off the bookshelf.

'Wait a minute,' said Chikashi, the voice of reason. 'What's the point of taking that thing? It's the cassette recorder you use to listen to the tapes Goro sent you, right? That's exactly the sort of absurd behaviour that always infuriates you when somebody else does it.'

2

Even in his late fifties, Kogito still took the streetcar to the pool, and he had noticed that he was usually the only person on board with an old-fashioned cassette recorder. Once in a while he would see a middle-aged man listening to a tape and moving his lips, from which Kogito deduced that the man must be practising English conversation. Until recently, the streetcars had been teeming with crowds of youths listening to music on their Walkmans, but now those same kids were all busy chatting on mobile phones or nimbly typing text messages on the tiny keyboards. Kogito actually felt nostalgic for the days when the tinny cacophony of popular music used to leak out of the young people's ubiquitous headphones, even though it had seemed annoying at the time. Nowadays, he concealed his bulky pre-Walkman recorder in the gym bag with his swimming equipment and wore the oversized headphones clamped around his greying head.

The old-fashioned cassette recorder had originally been given to Goro, back in the days when he was still working as an actor, as a perk for appearing in a TV commercial for an electronics company. The recording device itself was just a common rectangular parallelepiped, but while the design of the machine was absolutely ordinary, the shape of the large, black, ear-covering headphones bore a curious resemblance to the giant medieval-armoured water beetles known as *tagame*, pronounced 'taga-may', that Kogito used to catch in the mountain streams when he was a boy in the forests of Shikoku. As he told Goro, the first time he tried using the headphones he felt as if, after all this time, he suddenly had a couple of those perpetually useless beetles fastened on to both sides of his head, crushing his skull like a vice.

But Goro said coolly, 'That just tells me that you were a kid who couldn't catch anything worthwhile like eels or freshwater trout, so you had to be satisfied with those grotesque bugs. I know it's a little late, but in any case, this is a gift from me to the pitiful little boy you used to be. You can call it Tagame or whatever, and maybe it'll cheer that poor kid up, retroactively.'

Goro seemed to think, somehow, that the cassette recorder alone wasn't a sufficiently grand gift for Kogito, who was not only an old friend but also his younger sister's husband. That was probably why, along with the cassette recorder, he also gave Kogito a very attractive miniature trunk, made of Duralumin – an item that demonstrated Goro's genius for assembling interesting little props, whether to enhance his personal lifestyle or to add atmospheric complexity to one of his films. And in that beguiling mini-trunk were twenty-five cassette tapes.

Goro presented Kogito with this quadripartite gift (trunk, cassette recorder, headphones, tapes) one evening after they had both attended a sneak preview of one of Goro's films at a large movie theatre in downtown Tokyo. Afterwards, riding home alone on the train, Kogito stuck one of the cassettes, each of which was identified only by a number stamped on a white label, into Tagame – for he had, in fact, already started to call the machine by the nickname Goro had suggested.

As Kogito was fumbling around, trying to insert the headphone plug into the appropriate jack, he must have inadvertently hit the play button, or perhaps there was a feature that automatically started playback when you inserted a tape. In any case, his fellow passengers in the tightly packed train car looked extremely startled when a loud, brassy-sounding female voice suddenly began to emanate from the vicinity of Kogito's lap. 'Aaah!' the woman shrieked through the tiny speaker. 'Oh my God! I think my uterus is falling out! Oh, no, I'm gonna come! Oh my God! I'm coming! Aaaaaah!'

As Kogito learned later, that tape was one of twenty similarly sensational recordings made by illegal electronic surveillance. Goro, who had a taste for such things, had been talked into buying the tapes by a colleague at a certain movie studio, and he had been wondering how to dispose of them. Since he seemed to consider loosening Kogito up to be one of his missions in life, Goro mischievously decided to bequeath the collection of 'blue tapes' to his bookish brother-in-law.

Earlier in his life, Kogito wouldn't have had the slightest interest in such sordid diversions, but at this particular time he threw himself into listening to the illicit recordings non-stop, over a hundred-day period, with a zeal bordering on mania. As it happened, Kogito was going through a rough patch in his life, and he had found himself plunged into an abyss of anxiety and depression. When Goro heard about this from Chikashi, he apparently said, 'In that case, maybe he needs a little hair of the dog, so to speak. When you're dealing with humanity in its coarsest, most vulgar form – I'm talking about that scumbag journalist – the best antidote is more of the same.' Kogito heard about

Goro's prescription from Chikashi, after the fact, but she remained blissfully ignorant of the contents of the tapes.

Kogito's depression had been brought on by a series of vicious ad hominem attacks on him by the 'scumbag journalist' Goro had mentioned, who was the star writer for a major newspaper. Needless to say, the highly personal criticisms of Kogito and his work – attacks that had been going on for more than a decade – were presented as the solemn discharge of the journalist's civic and professional duty.

As long as Kogito was busy reading and working on various writing projects, he didn't think much about his widely published enemy's vendetta against him. But late at night when he suddenly found himself wide awake, or when he was out walking around town on some errand or other, the peculiarly abusive words of his nemesis (who was a talented writer, no question about it) kept running through his head like toxic sludge.

Even though the reporter was known for being meticulous in his newspaper work, when he sat down to compose his poison-pen missives to Kogito he would take dirty-looking, mistake-ridden manuscript pages and smudged faxes of galley proofs, cut them up into small pieces, scribble unpleasant 'greetings' on those grubby scraps of recycled paper, and then mail them to Kogito's home address along with copies of the journalist's own books and magazine articles, many of which were obsessively devoted to Kogito-bashing.

In spite of himself, Kogito would immediately commit every word of the loathsome tirades to memory, but whenever it looked as if one of his enemy's vitriolic insults might be about to pollute his brain again, all he had to do to calm himself down, whether he was lying in bed in his study, or out and about in Tokyo, was to don his headphones and listen to the honest voices of 'vulgar humanity'. As Goro put it, 'It's really astonishing the way listening to trashy stuff like that can take your mind off whatever's bothering you.'

Fifteen years went by, and one day Kogito was packing for an overseas trip. While he was searching for some of the research material he needed to take with him, his eyes happened to light on the miniature

Duralumin trunk tucked away in a corner of his study. Over the years he had turned it into a repository for the libellous books and articles that were constantly being delivered from his nemesis, the accursed journalist, but it still held those electronic eavesdropping tapes as well. What if his plane crashed, and Chikashi happened to listen to those steamy tapes while she was putting his affairs in order posthumously? To avoid that potential catastrophe, he tossed the tapes into the trash and then asked Chikashi to find out whether the little brushed aluminium trunk was something Goro might like to have returned.

Goro apparently said yes, and so it was that the Duralumin trunk found its way back to its original owner. But then, after another two or three years had passed, the same elegant container turned up at Kogito's house again while he was abroad, teaching in Boston. This time it was packed with a batch of thirty or so different cassettes, not lurid surveillance soundtracks this time, but rather tapes of Goro rambling on about various topics. Goro explained to Chikashi that he would be sending new recordings as soon as he got them finished, with the goal of eventually filling the container to its fifty-tape capacity. When Goro mentioned that the contents were nothing urgent, Chikashi replied jokingly that since Kogito was approaching the age where he could soon begin losing his mental acuity, she might suggest that he save the tapes for his dotage.

But when Kogito returned from the United States and saw the new batch of tapes, he was seized by a vague but insistent premonition and immediately popped one of them into Tagame. As Kogito had suspected, the voice that came booming through the headphones belonged to Goro, and it soon became evident that the purpose of the tapes was to tell the story, in no particular chronological order, of the things that had happened to Kogito and Goro after they became friends at school in the Shikoku town of Matsuyama – 'Mat'chama', in Goro's idiosyncratic pronunciation.

Goro's way of speaking on the tapes wasn't a monologue, exactly. Rather, it was as if he and Kogito were having an extended conversation on the telephone. Because of this, Kogito soon got into the habit of listening to the tapes before he went to sleep in his study. Lying on his side with the headphones on, he would listen to the recordings while a host of thoughts floated languidly through his mind.

As new tapes continued to arrive at regular intervals, Kogito would listen to each one, and then, almost as if they were having a real-time conversation, he would punctuate Goro's recorded remarks from time to time by pressing the pause button and giving voice to his own opinions. That practice quickly turned into a routine, and before long, even though Goro couldn't hear Kogito's responses, communicating by way of Tagame ended up almost entirely replacing their occasional phone chats.

On the night in question, a few hours before he learned that Goro had plunged to his death from the roof of his production company's office building in an upmarket section of Tokyo, Kogito was indulging in his customary bedtime ritual: lying in bed listening to the latest tape, which had been delivered by courier earlier that evening. While Goro rambled eloquently along, Kogito would stop the tape whenever the impulse struck him and interpolate – not so much his own views any more, but rather his natural, spontaneous conversational responses to whatever Goro might be saying. What Kogito remembered about that evening's session, in retrospect, is that he was suddenly struck with the idea of buying a cassette recorder with editing capabilities, which would allow him to cobble together a third tape that incorporated both sides of his lively and occasionally contentious 'dialogues' with Goro.

At one point there was a stretch of silence on the tape, and when Goro began talking again his voice sounded very different. It was immediately clear from his blurry diction that he'd had a few drinks during the break, and had forgotten to stop the tape. 'So anyway, that's it for today – I'm going to head over to the Other Side now,' Goro said, quite casually.

After that declaration, there was a sound that Kogito eventually came to think of as the Terrible Thud. It was the sort of dramatic embellishment you would expect from a high-tech film-maker like Goro, who was known for his skilful use of sound effects and composite recordings. Only later did Kogito realize that the thud was the sound you might hear when a heavy body fell from a high place and crashed on to the unyielding pavement below: *Ka-thunk*.

'But don't worry,' Goro went on, 'I'm not going to stop communicating with you. That's why I made a special point of setting up this system with Tagame and the tapes. Well, I know it's probably getting late on *your* side. Goodnight!' he concluded cheerfully, in a voice that bore no trace of intoxication.

Kogito actually thought, more than once, that maybe that portentous announcement ('I'm going to head over to the Other Side now') was the last thing Goro said before he jumped, intentionally pre-recorded to serve as his final words, and the remarks that followed the thud, made by a totally sober-sounding Goro, were the first dispatch from the Other Side, using the Tagame cassette recorder as a sort of interdimensional mobile phone. If that was true, then if Kogito just went on listening to the tapes using the same system, shouldn't he be able to hear Goro's voice from the Other Side? And so he continued his bedtime ritual of chatting with Goro almost every night, via the medium of Tagame, running through the collection of tapes in no particular order – except for the final tape, which he put away in the trunk without bothering to rewind.

3

Kogito and Chikashi arrived at Goro's house in the seaside town of Yugawara just as the body was being brought home from the police station, but Kogito managed to avoid seeing his dead friend's face. There was a small private wake, after which Umeko, Goro's widow (who had starred in many of Goro's films), planned to stay up all night watching videos of Goro's movies with anyone who wanted to join her. Kogito explained that he needed to get back to Tokyo to take care of Akari, their son, who had been left at home alone, and it was decided that Chikashi would stay in Yugawara and attend her brother's cremation the following day.

Glancing towards the coffin, Umeko said, 'I could hardly recognize

Goro's face when I saw it at the police station, but now he's back to looking like his handsome self again. Please take a peek and pay your respects.'

In response to this, Chikashi said to Kogito, in a quiet but powerful voice, 'Actually, I think it would be better if you didn't look.'

Meeting Umeko's quizzical eyes, Chikashi returned her sister-in-law's gaze with a look of absolute conviction and candour, overlaid with sadness. Umeko clearly understood, and she stood up and went into the room with the coffin, alone.

Kogito, meanwhile, was thinking about how distant he had felt from Chikashi while she was staring at Umeko with that strong, defiant expression. There was absolutely no trace, in Chikashi's utterly direct look, of the genteel social buffers that usually softened her speech and conduct. *This is the way it is, and there's nothing we can do about it*, Chikashi seemed to be trying to tell herself as well, in the midst of her overwhelming grief and sorrow. *It's fine for Umeko to gaze lovingly at the destroyed face of Goro's corpse and imagine, wishfully, that those dead features have been miraculously restored to their original handsome, animated form. As his sister, I'm doing exactly the same thing. But I think seeing Goro's face would just be too much for Kogito to bear.*

As Chikashi perceptively surmised, the prospect of viewing Goro's dead body filled Kogito with dread, but when Umeko voiced her request he automatically started to stand up. He couldn't help thinking that he would never be mature enough to handle something like this, and he was engulfed by feelings of loneliness and isolation. But he was conscious of another motivation for agreeing to view the corpse as well: he was curious to see whether there might be a mark stretching along Goro's cheek that would indicate he had been talking into a Tagame-type headset when he jumped. The impact, Kogito theorized, could have left an imprint that would still be visible now, and he had reason to believe that scenario wasn't merely his own wild conjecture.

Taruto, who was the head of Goro's production company as well as the CEO of his own family-owned company in Shikoku, had taken on the task of transporting Goro's body to Yugawara, and after the wake he showed the family some things he had found on Goro's desk at the office. Along with three different versions of a suicide note, written on a personal computer, there was a drawing done in soft pencil on high-quality, watermarked paper.

The picture, which was drawn in a style reminiscent of an illustrated book of fairy tales from some unspecified foreign country, showed a late-middle-aged man floating through a sky populated with innumerable clouds that resembled French dinner rolls. The man's position reminded Kogito of the way Akari sprawled out on the floor whenever he was composing music, and this added to Kogito's immediate certainty that the picture was a self-portrait of Goro. Furthermore, the man who was wafting through the air was holding a mobile phone that looked very much like a miniature version of Tagame in his left hand, and talking into it. (Hence Kogito's suspicion that there might have been a headset mark on Goro's dead face.)

4

Kogito left the house of mourning in Yugawara and headed for the Japan Railways station, planning to board an express train for Tokyo. But the moment he walked into the station he was besieged by an unruly horde of TV reporters and photographers who had obviously been lying in wait, eager to talk to anyone with the slightest connection to the late Goro Hanawa.

Ignoring the shouted questions, Kogito tried to steer clear of the ring of jostling reporters, but then a rapidly revolving TV camera collided with the lower part of the bridge of his nose, barely missing his right eye. The young cameraman looked at Kogito with an insolent half-smile; he might just have been covering up his distress and confusion with a facade of arrogance, but Kogito felt that his facial expression was very crass and inappropriate indeed.

After escaping from the mob scene at the train station, Kogito started walking up a long, narrow lane that had been carved out of a hillside of mandarin orange trees and paved with cobblestones. At the top of the slope he found a taxi and climbed in. The driver must have been acquainted with Goro, because he took one look at Kogito and said, 'I guess it's really true what they say about crying tears of blood!' It was only then that Kogito realized that half of his face was covered with blood from the deep cut on his nose.

Even so, he felt that rushing to the nearest emergency room and getting the paperwork to prove that he had been injured, as a way of punishing that arrogant cameraman, would have been an overreaction. Besides, the cameraman was just the inadvertent point man for that seething mass of journalists, with their insatiable collective appetite for tragedy and scandal. In the short time since Goro's death, Kogito had received a very distinct impression from all the media people, whether they were with television networks, newspapers or weekly tabloid magazines: that is, he had noticed that they all seemed to share a kind of contemptuous scorn for anyone who had committed suicide. At the root of that contempt seemed to be the feeling that Goro, who had for years been lionized, lauded, and treated like royalty by the media, had somehow betrayed them, almost on a personal level, and as a result the fallen idol could never again be restored to his previous kingly status.

For about a week after Goro's suicide, Kogito made a point of watching the *Wide News* programme early every morning and again in the evening. Since no one else in his household showed the slightest interest in joining him, he would carry the small TV set into his study and put it at the foot of his bed, then listen to the sound through his Tagame headphones.

Kogito had expected that he might have difficulty understanding the speech of the younger generation: that is, the anchors and reporters on the news shows, and the actors (male and female) who had appeared in Goro's films. But he even found it hard to follow the remarks of the film directors and screenwriters, not to mention the commentators from the arts and from the larger world beyond, who were more or less his own age. And the harder Kogito concentrated on trying to understand what all these talking heads were saying, the more incomprehensible their babble became.

Meanwhile, Kogito developed a new habit – an addiction, really –

which he was keeping secret from Chikashi. He had surreptitiously resumed the lively dialogues with Tagame that he had been engaging in, off and on, during the three months preceding Goro's suicide, with the army cot in his study as the staging ground. Only now he was doing it on a more serious and a more regular basis than before – that is to say, daily.

Since Goro's suicide, Kogito had made a rule about how these midnight conversations with Tagame were to be conducted, and he was very conscientious about following that arbitrary regulation to the letter.

The rule was: Never mention the fact that Goro has gone to the Other Side. This was easier said than done, of course, and at the beginning, whenever Kogito was chatting away with (or at) Tagame, he was unable to erase Goro's suicide from his mind for even a moment. Before too long, though, new ideas just naturally began to bubble up. For one thing, Kogito was intensely curious about the Other Side, where Goro had now resided. In terms of space and time, was it completely different from the world on this side? And when you were there, looking back across the existential divide, would the very fact of your death on this side be nullified, as if you had never died at all?

Before Kogito met Goro at Matsuyama High School, he had been thinking about what certain philosophers had written on the various types of death perception, but there hadn't been anyone he could talk to about such things. Not long after he and Goro became friends, he broached the subject. In those days – and, now that he thought about it, throughout their long association – their basic style of communication had been infused with jokiness and wordplay, and they tended to aim for humorous effect even when they were discussing profoundly serious matters.

Naturally, it was inevitable that young Kogito would always take a position contrary to those expressed in the rather staid language of the philosophy books he was reading. To wit:

It goes without saying that someone who is living in this world wouldn't be able to talk knowledgeably about his own death, based on first-hand experience. That's because the essence of intelligent consciousness ceases to be at the same moment that one's actual existence is coming to an end. In other words, for people who are alive and living, death simply doesn't exist, and by the time they experience it directly they're already beyond cognitive understanding.

Kogito began by quoting that argument, which he had read somewhere, and then proceeded to outline his own interpretative variation on the theme.

'Let's say there is such a thing as a human soul, and it's alive, along with the body it inhabits. In my village, there's a folk belief that when someone dies – that is, when a person ceases to exist in a physical form – the soul leaves the body and goes up into the air of the valley, spinning around in a spiral movement, like a tornado. (The valley is shaped rather like the inside of a wide-mouthed jar, and the soul doesn't venture beyond those confines.) At some point the disembodied spirit reverses its corkscrew trajectory and returns to earth, landing at the base of a tree high up on one of the heavily wooded mountainsides that enclose the valley – not just any old tree, but a specific one that has been selected beforehand by karma, or fate. Then, when the moment is right, the old soul will make its way down to the village and find a home in the body of a newborn baby.'

Goro responded to this bit of folklore with an esoteric reference that showcased his own precociously sophisticated store of knowledge. 'According to Dante,' he declared, 'the right way for a human being to climb a mountain is by going around to the right, and if you take the left-hand route you could be making a big mistake. When a spirit spirals from your valley up into the forest, which way is it moving: clockwise, or counterclockwise?'

His grandmother hadn't shared that logistical detail, so instead of giving a straightforward answer Kogito ventured a wild surmise, half in jest: 'I guess that would depend on how people used to think about birth, and death. If they thought it was *bad* when the soul left an old body and went to the root of a tree, and *good* when that same soul entered into the body of a newborn baby, then I guess the spiral would be clockwise in the case of rebirth, and counterclockwise for death.'

Then he added, 'Seriously, though, if the soul is able to detach itself from the body in that way, then the spirit must not be aware that it's dead. So what dies is just the body, and at the moment when the flesh ceases to be alive the spirit goes its own way. In other words, the spirit goes on living forever, divorced from the body's finite sense of time and space. To tell you the truth, I don't really understand it myself, so I'm groping around for an explanation. But I think that just as there's infinity and also a single instant in time, and just as the entire cosmos can coexist with a single particle, isn't it possible that when we die we simply move into a different dimension of space and time? If that's the case, then maybe the soul could continue existing in a fourth-dimensional state of innocent bliss, without ever noticing that there's such a thing as death.'

And now that giddy, carefree, existential conversation they had enjoyed on that day in their youth, having more fun fooling around with the high-flown words than with the actual concepts – now, that seemingly abstract scenario had really come to pass. And here was Goro's spirit, lively as ever, talking to Kogito through Tagame as if he truly hadn't noticed that his mortal body had already gone up in smoke.

5

Late that night, on the day after Goro took his leap into the next dimension, Kogito finally made it home with the bloodstained handkerchief still pressed against the TV-camera gash between his eyes. He made dinner for Akari, who had been listening to CDs with the answering machine on and the telephone ringer silenced, and then, after washing his injured face (he kept the light in the bathroom turned off and didn't even glance at himself in the mirror), Kogito trudged up the stairs to his study.

Of course, Kogito was always the one who started the conversations with Tagame, but sometimes, just before he pressed the play button, he had the uncanny feeling that the chunky little cassette recorder was actually psyching itself up for the next round of combat.

For some reason this made Kogito think about the way the real *tagames* – the large, oddly shaped water beetles that lived in the mountain streams of Shikoku – must have amorously bestirred themselves, almost in slow motion, during mating season. All these years later, that image (which may have been pure conjecture) was perfectly sharp and vivid in his mind.

Kogito always left the tape cued up at the end of the previous night's conversation, and whenever he picked Tagame up he always felt as if he were answering an incoming call on the ultimate long-distance mobile phone. And the moment Goro's voice began to speak, with its distinctive Kyoto/Matsuyama accent, Kogito was repeatedly struck by the fact that whatever the topic might turn out to be, it always seemed to be uncannily relevant to his current situation.

Another odd thing was that when he started talking to Tagame, Kogito was far more enthusiastic than he had been about any other kind of discussion with Goro during the past twenty years or so. There was something engaging about Goro's relaxed way of talking across the boundaries that separated the Other Side from the land of the living – despite the fact that his comments often consisted of merciless, searing criticism of Kogito – and even though Kogito was completely aware that Goro was dead, the intensity of their exchanges somehow seemed to overshadow that disturbing fact.

Kogito also felt that he had been forced to take another look at his feelings about his own inevitable death, so naturally there were times when the conversations evoked newly urgent thoughts about what really happens after we die. He could imagine himself, in the not so distant future, travelling to the Other Side with an upgraded, afterlife-appropriate version of Tagame and earnestly awaiting a dispatch from this side. When he thought that there might be no answer to his Tagame signals, for all eternity, he felt such a deep sense of loneliness and desolation that his entire being seemed to be disintegrating.

At the same time, it was only natural for him to feel that the impassioned 'conversations' he was carrying on with Tagame, all by himself, were nothing but an escapist diversion, a self-deluding mind game. As a novelist who'd grown partial to the literary theories espoused by Mikhail Bakhtin, Kogito had started to take the concept of 'playing games' very seriously after crossing the threshold into middle age. Consequently, he knew very well that even if talking with Goro via Tagame was a mere diversion, as long as he was acting on that fantasy stage there was nothing to do but throw himself into the part with all his heart.

Furthermore, Kogito resolved that during the day, while he was separated from Tagame, he wouldn't allow his nocturnal conversations with Goro to seep into his daily experiences. And when he was talking about Goro with Chikashi, or with Umeko, or with Taruto, Kogito made every effort not to recall the conversations with Goro that flowed through Tagame.

In this way, Kogito constructed a barrier between the two types of time – real time and Tagame time – and while he was moving around in one zone he wouldn't permit the other to spill over into it, or vice versa. But whichever zone he happened to be inhabiting, he never denied, at least not to his innermost self, the truth or the reality of what he had experienced in the other realm. From his vantage point on the earthly, conscious side, he firmly believed in the existence of the Other Side, and that belief made the world on this side seem infinitely deeper and richer. Even if his Tagame adventure was nothing but a dream, he still embraced it as a positive experience.

6

One year, Kogito was invited to speak at Kyushu University. While he was in the green room waiting for his lecture to begin, he happened to glance at a timetable and discovered that if he skipped the banquet with the other participants and hopped on the next ferry to Shikoku, then transferred to a Japan Railways train, he could be back at his childhood home, deep in the forest, before the night was over. He asked the assistant professor who was looking after him to make the travel arrangements, and the tickets were purchased while Kogito was delivering his lecture.

By the time Kogito made his way to the house where he was born, it was after eleven p.m. and his mother had already gone to sleep. The next morning, Kogito was up early. When he peered down the covered passageway that led to an adjoining bungalow, he could see the silhouette of his naked mother, illuminated by the reflected river-dazzle that leaked into the dark parlour through the gaps in the wooden rain shutters. Backlit like that, Kogito's mother looked almost like a young girl as (with the help of her sister-in-law) she twined the turban she always wore in public around her head. At that moment, his mother didn't seem to belong entirely to this world; it was as if she had already begun to make the transition over to the Other Side. Her abnormally large ear, which resembled a fish's dorsal fin, was hanging down from her emaciated profile, almost as if that misshapen appendage itself was absorbed in deep meditation.

Later, when they were sitting across from each other at the breakfast table, Kogito's mother began to speak in the local Iyo dialect, which tends to feature more exclamatory sentences than standard Japanese. 'I've been praying for a chance to see you since the beginning of last spring, Kogito!' she began. (It was already fall.) 'And now that you're sitting here, I still half feel as if it's my fantasy eating breakfast in front of me. It doesn't help that I can barely hear what you're saying, of course. I've gotten quite deaf, and on top of that you still don't open your mouth wide enough when you speak, just like when you were a child!

'But anyway, right now I feel as if this is half reality and half fanciful daydream! Besides, lately, no matter what's going on, I'm never entirely certain that it's really happening! When I was wishing that I could see you, it almost seemed as though half of you was already here. At times like that, if I voiced my opinions to you out loud, the other people in the house would just laugh indulgently. However, if you happened to be on television talking about something and I said to the TV set, "You're wrong about that, you know," even my great-grandchild would jump in and try to stop me, saying, "That's rude to Uncle Kogito." They think it's amusing when I talk to an invisible person, but isn't the television itself a kind of fantastical illusion? Just because there's no machine attached to my private hallucinations, does that make them any less "real" than the images on TV? I mean, what's the basis for that kind of thinking?

'Anyway, it seems as if almost everything is already an apparition to me, you know? Everyday life seems like television, and I can't tell whether somebody is really here with me or not. I'm surrounded by apparitions. One day soon I, too, will stop being real, and I'll become nothing more than a phantasm myself! But this valley has always been swarming with spectres, so I may not even notice when I make the shift over to the Other Side.'

After Kogito finished his breakfast, his younger sister gave him a ride to Matsuyama Airport so he could catch a plane that left before noon. When his sister called Chikashi in Tokyo to report that Kogito's departure had gone according to plan, she added, 'As Mother was nodding off after breakfast, she said, "A little while ago I saw an apparition of Kogito, and we had a nice chat." '

When he heard this story later, Kogito felt unexpectedly moved by his mother's remark. After committing suicide, Goro hadn't really noticed that he'd left this world and become a spirit on the Other Side, had he? When he thought about it that way, Kogito came to see the fluidity between the two dimensions as a positive thing, especially late at night, after he'd been talking to Goro through the magical medium of Tagame.

7

One day during the period when Kogito was indulging in long, intense Tagame dialogues on a nightly basis, Chikashi cornered him and, typically, burst out with a torrent of words that had obviously been germinating in her mind for quite a while.

'After all this time,' she began, 'when I hear you carrying on in your study every evening into the wee hours, complaining to Goro and then seeming to strain your ears for a response, I can't help wondering whether this isn't exactly the sort of "absurdity" you dislike so much.

I don't see what good can possibly come of indulging in this sort of charade night after night, and I'm really at my wits' end. Every time I hear you talking so impassionedly to Goro I can sense that you're waiting for a reply, and I know it must be terribly painful for you. I sympathize completely, and I truly do feel sorry for you. It's the same as if by some chance you suddenly died in an accident or something. I think about how puzzled and devastated Akari would be, and how sorry I'd feel for him. It isn't that I think you're doing these late-night seances as a way of gearing up for your own journey to the Other Side, but still…

'In any case, because your study is right above our bedrooms, it's really hard on us when your voice comes floating down. It's a bit like water dripping slowly through a bamboo strainer, and I think it's probably bothering Akari even more than me. No matter how low you keep your voice, and even when it's obvious that you're just listening to Goro's tapes on your headphones, I don't think it's possible for Akari to simply ignore what's going on. So I'm just wondering whether you might be willing to put an end to your sessions, for us?'

And then while Kogito watched, appalled, Chikashi unexpectedly began to cry. He had no choice but to admit that for these past few months he had been so engrossed in living by the Rule of Tagame that he had forgotten that there were rules about living as part of a family, too. On another level, he had been startled by the aside Chikashi had tossed out in the middle of her speech: *It isn't that I think you're doing these late-night seances as a way of gearing up for your own journey to the Other Side, but still…*

8

'But I just can't do that!' Kogito wailed. He was alone in his study, lying face down on his army cot with the sheets pulled tightly over his head, talking to himself. 'I know my behaviour has been shameful, getting so immersed in Tagame to the point where it's become a kind of crazy obsession. But there's another person involved in this. I can't very well just announce, unilaterally, "Sorry, pal, it's over." Think about poor

Goro, all alone on the Other Side. How terrible would that be for him?'

Kogito got up, switched on the light and pulled the Duralumin trunk out from under the bed. He had just remembered something Goro had said on one of the tapes, and now, using his own topical annotations on the labels as a guide, he found the tape in question, popped it into Tagame and hastily cued up the relevant passage. Then, as if urged on by the slow, whirring vibration of the cassette recorder, he gave a decisive nod and pressed the play button.

'Of course, you're always like this,' Goro's voice began, ragging on Kogito right out of the gate. 'But from what I hear these days, true to form, you've been acting like a mouse trapped in a bag. When you get right down to it, you've brought all your suffering on yourself, and now you're floundering around helplessly. Chikashi's been complaining to me, you know,' Goro went on. 'She says that same big-shot scumbag journalist has been denouncing you again, in the nastiest, most contemptible way. That vendetta has already been dragging on for twenty-five years now. Don't you think it's time for you to let it go?

'Lately you've been in pretty low spirits, and you've brought Chikashi and Akari down as well. There's no way you can say that's a good thing. Even without having to cope with a depressed husband, Chikashi is someone who's experienced more than her fair share of hard times. When the busybodies say that your family appears to have a pretty cushy life, you should just reply that the pleasant things pass soon enough, as if they'd never happened, but the painful experiences tend to linger on for a long, long time.

'The sort of person who's forever revelling in every little delight with an excessive, borderline-abnormal kind of euphoria, and who does nothing but cling to those lovely airbrushed memories: that, in my opinion, is a thoroughly unhappy and unfortunate person. Chikashi has been through far too much suffering already, but in spite of that she has never turned into the sort of weak person who's always longing to return to happier days. Don't you agree?

'Anyway, I've been thinking about your situation, and I was wondering, how would it be if you took a little breather and left town for a while? You've been toiling away at the novelist's life for all these years, and I really think you could use some quarantine time right about now. I think if you just got away from your novels for a while... If you left for good it would be rough on Chikashi and Akari, that's why I say "for a while". What I mean is, you need to impose a quarantine on yourself and take a break from the sort of life where you're being confronted by the distressing gutter journalism of this country on a daily basis.'

'Give me a minute to check something in the dictionary,' Kogito replied. 'When you first mentioned this, some time ago, I had a passing familiarity with the word "quarantine", so I didn't take the time to look it up and find out exactly what it meant. But the word hasn't taken root in my mind to the point where I would actually use it.'

After pressing the pause button, Kogito brought out one of his dictionaries and flipped the pages until he found what he was looking for:

> **quarantine** (kwor-an-teen) *n.* 1. A state, period, or place of isolation in which people or animals that have arrived from elsewhere or been exposed to infectious or contagious diseases are placed. *v.* [with object] to put a person or animal in quarantine. 2. *n.* The period of this isolation. Origin: mid–17th century, from Italian *quarantina*, 'forty days', from *quaranta*, 'forty'.

After he had finished reading those definitions, Kogito turned back to Tagame, making an effort to keep his voice as low as possible while simultaneously striving to pronounce every word with perfect clarity. 'Listen, Goro,' he said, before pressing the play button again. 'I know you're using this word to try to advance a certain agenda, and I understand exactly what you're driving at.'

'Of course, it doesn't have to be exactly forty days,' responded Goro's recorded voice. 'You might have a chance to stay away longer. But what do you think about Berlin as a temporary haven, to put some distance between you and that journalist? (On the bright side, *he* isn't getting any younger, either!) For me at least, Berlin is an unforgettable place. If someone asked me what connection that city might have with your self-imposed quarantine, I couldn't say exactly, but…'

'Berlin, eh? Now that you mention it, I did receive an invitation to go there, for considerably longer than forty days!' Kogito exclaimed, hearing the surprise and excitement in his own voice, which had grown suddenly loud as he momentarily forgot about the need to whisper. 'I'll check now, but I think the offer's still good.'

Whereupon Kogito stopped the tape and went to his study to look for the file in question. S. Fischer Verlag (the publisher who had brought out the first German translations of Kogito's early novels) was still doing so, even though sales weren't what they used to be. Every few years – or, more usually, every ten or twelve years – a new translation of one of Kogito's novels would come out in hardcover, but as a rule the subsequent printings would be in paperback. Whenever Kogito gave readings at places such as the Frankfurt Book Fair or cultural associations in Hamburg and Munich, there would be a book signing afterwards, where they were always able to sell quite a few of the colourful, beautifully designed paperbacks of his work. And now he had been offered a lectureship at the Berlin Free University to commemorate S. Fischer, the founder of the eponymous publishing house. The course was to begin in the middle of November, so he still had time to accept. The department's offer was generous, and they even said that they would keep the slot open for him through the first half of the term.

By the time he climbed back into bed, Kogito had dug up the most recent fax from a secretary in S. Fischer Verlag's editorial division and learned that he still had three days to let them know whether he wanted to accept the position of guest lecturer at the Free University. To his own amazement, in a matter of a few minutes he had made up his mind to take Goro's rather drastic advice and get out of town for a while.

The tape on which Goro suggested a 'quarantine' had been recorded several months earlier, but now his casual suggestion had become a necessity, for a different reason: namely, Kogito's need to pull himself together and get over his addiction to talking to Goro through Tagame. Even after Chikashi's heartfelt complaint, earlier that evening, Kogito hadn't been able to leave the cassette recorder on the bookshelf for even this one night. And as it turned out it was Goro, his Tagame partner, who had dropped the hint that had galvanized him into positive action. Somehow, mixed in with his decision to make a bold move, Kogito felt a resurgence of his old dependence on Goro.

He was just about to ask, 'What's going to become of our sessions with Tagame?' But then, without pressing the play button, he answered his own question. Or, to put it more precisely, he consciously crafted a response along the lines of what he thought Goro might have said in real life: *That's for you to decide. But when Chikashi criticized your behaviour last night, rather than any annoyance or inconvenience to her and Akari, she was probably more concerned about finding a way to free you from your addiction to our Tagame sessions, don't you think?*

9

Nevertheless, right up until the night before he was scheduled to leave for wintry Berlin, Kogito was unable to give up his nightly ritual of talking to Goro by way of Tagame – although he did, at least, make every effort to keep his voice low. The thing was, when he told Chikashi the next day about his decision to go into Tagame-free quarantine in Berlin, she naturally interpreted this action as a direct response to her request: a way for Kogito to take a break from his 'seances' with Goro. That being the case, no matter how much he lowered his voice, Chikashi was probably still aware that the conversations were continuing, but because the end was in sight her silence on the matter seemed to constitute a sort of tacit approval, or at least forbearance.

Then one morning, as Kogito's departure date was rapidly approaching, Chikashi (who had been busying herself every evening with packing and repacking his trunk) said, 'Last night I felt like going through Goro's letters, and I came across a watercolour painting that he sent from Berlin. Would you like to see it? It's a landscape, on lovely paper. It's actually drawn with coloured pencils, then blurred with a wet brush so it ends up looking like a watercolour. The painting seems to have a really buoyant, happy feeling. On the back is written THIS MORNING IS THE ONLY DAY THAT'S BEEN THIS CLEAR SINCE I'VE BEEN HERE, and on the front, in the lower corner, is Goro's signature.'

Kogito looked at the landscape painting, which was on soft, thick, pale-sepia paper with slightly ragged edges, like a pricey wedding invitation. In classic Goro-style, the paper had been roughly torn into a rectangular shape. The centrepiece of the composition was a huge tree, seen from above: stout trunk, bare treetops, and a chaotic tangle of leafless branches with attenuated tips, all minutely detailed in such a way as to delineate the subtleties of light and shade amid the homogeneous hues of grey and brown. The only green came from the perennial creepers that snaked around the tree trunk, while patches of deep blue sky thickly sprinkled with fluffy white clouds could be glimpsed through the lacy jumble of bare, thin branches.

'Goro must have wanted to paint that sky because it was such a gorgeous colour,' Chikashi said. 'I remember he told me on the phone that Berlin was cloudy every day, from morning on, and then it got dark around four p.m. He said things like, "Berlin in winter isn't a fit place for a human being." But that makes it seem even more remarkable that this painting is so bright and full of life. He was probably walking around the city when an unusual set of coloured pencils in an art supply store caught his eye, and he just bought them on the spur of the moment. And then, when he was looking out his hotel window at the first clear sky since he'd arrived, he suddenly felt like painting it...' ■

CALL ME BY MY PROPER NAME

Rupert Thomson

M y mother's brother was christened Cedric, but people always called him Joe. As a child, I don't remember seeing Uncle Joe, not even once. All kinds of stories were told about him, though. A brilliant scholar, of whom great things were expected, he was expelled from public school in Tonbridge for taking a group of younger boys to the cinema in Maidstone. In his early twenties, he was offered a job by the London Bank of South America. He flew to Colombia. Within a few months of landing in Bogotá, he moved out of the approved lodgings for single employees and registered in a hotel under an assumed identity. He had sex with local women. He grew a beard. The bank transferred him to a less prestigious branch in Ecuador. A year later, in circumstances that had never been entirely clear to me, Joe was deported. Back in England, he joined the army, but since his superiors at the bank had only given him a one-line reference, stating merely that he had been in their employ, he wasn't considered officer material. Sent out to Korea, he managed to avoid active duty. He also managed to burn down a hut belonging to the regiment. On returning from the

Wendy, Frank, Pim and Joe in 1946, shortly before Joe was expelled from school

war, he worked down a coal mine, then in a petrol station on the A5. Later, he delivered milk. In his mid-forties, he took to his bed, sleeping naked in sheets that were soaked in olive oil. He claimed it was good for his skin. The beard grew again, longer this time. He lived on boiled rice and packets of Benson & Hedges. If family members tried to visit, he would tell them to bugger off. Most years, a Christmas card would arrive at our house, signed simply 'Uncle Joe', or he would send a mouldy bar of chocolate, which would immediately be consigned to the dustbin, but Joe himself remained an enigma. The few facts I was able to gather only made him harder to imagine; he seemed to disappear behind them, as one might disappear behind a wig and a false nose. All Dad would ever say was that he was 'a bad influence', and that Wendy, our mother, had been frightened of him, and had avoided him; Dad seemed to worry that we, his sons, might have inherited Joe's genes, and might end up the same way. In the late Seventies, Joe's life took yet another turn, perhaps the most unlikely one of all: he became a Muslim. Suddenly he wasn't Cedric any more, or even Uncle Joe. He was Abdul Rauf.

In 1986, Joe's brother, my uncle Frank, offered to take me to see him. By then Joe was living in Wolverhampton, in a place called Penndale Lodge, which Frank gave me to understand was some sort of refuge for destitute old men. From Four Oaks, the private estate where Frank and my aunt Miriam lived, it was a forty-minute drive, and within a quarter of an hour of setting out the landscape began to deteriorate. During the nineteenth century, Wolverhampton had been a thriving industrial centre, with a huge steelworks, several well-established coach builders and a famous bicycle manufacturer – great fortunes had been made in the town – but now, on every side, there were boarded-up shops, derelict factories and vacant lots littered with builders' rubble and broken glass.

As we drove through this urban wasteland, I turned to Frank. 'I hadn't realized how run-down it was round here.'

'Oh, it's terrible,' he said, 'just *terrible.*'

He stopped in a suburb called Whitmore Reans, outside a scruffy grocery store whose sign was in Arabic. When he returned, he was clutching two brown-paper bags. He told me he had bought some things he thought Joe might appreciate.

After driving for a few more minutes, we turned into a narrow street of terraced housing. Penndale Lodge – the name was on the gatepost – had a dull red-brick facade and grubby windows, and its front door was painted a shade of blue that reminded me of the police. My stomach tightened, and in an attempt to quieten my nerves I started talking.

'It doesn't look much like a lodge to me.'

'I know.' Frank's eyebrows lifted until they were almost at right angles to each other, and his eyes squeezed shut. 'He just dragged himself down, Joe did. He was *determined* to drag himself down. All the way to the gutter.'

'You told me a story once, about the time he showed up on your doorstep. He'd been living rough, in Birmingham...'

'Did I?'

'He hadn't changed his clothes for weeks, apparently. He smelled awful.'

Miriam had told me that Joe had been wearing his underpants for so long that it was impossible to work out what colour they'd been when they were new.

'Yes.' Frank was nodding now, but with the same anguished expression. 'Yes, yes, I think that's right.'

My probing always seemed to put Frank under pressure. I was after details that would bring Joe to life, but these were the very details Frank concealed from himself. I imagined Joe must have been truly desperate to have thrown himself on his brother's mercy; in the stories I had heard, he came across as a proud man, somebody who would go to almost any lengths to avoid invoking pity or condescension. I recalled another snippet of information Frank had once let slip.

'He was diagnosed as a schizophrenic, wasn't he?'

'I think so,' Frank said wearily. 'I'm not sure. He was in the same hospital as Mummy for a while – St Andrew's, in Northampton.'

'When was that?'

'In the Fifties. Fifty-seven or -eight. I was in there too.'

I turned and looked at him. 'Were you? What for?'

'I had a breakdown. It was worrying about the mill that did it. Waiting to take over the mill, and Eric being such a bastard about it all.'

Eric was Frank's uncle – my great-uncle – and the mill was a family business that Eric used to own and run. Built out of smoke-blackened brick and dating from the early Victorian period, it had a flat roof, tottering chimneys and row upon row of tall, blind windows, and it backed on to a desolate, sleepy canal whose water was permanently hidden under a skin of pale-green algae. It took ninety women to operate the weaving machines, and I had always been intrigued by what they manufactured: the tape and webbing could be transformed into the loops in the back of a pair of boots, the edging of a horse blanket, or the straps on a rucksack or a parachute. As retirement approached, Eric had needed to start thinking about a successor. Since he had never married or had children, his eldest nephew, Frank, was the obvious choice, but Eric had constantly threatened to overlook him in favour of Norman, an epileptic he already employed in a minor managerial role. He would tell Frank how impressed he was with Norman, how Norman had what it took. Frank, he said, was 'nesh' – local slang for 'incompetent' or 'weak'. It seemed to amuse Eric to play the two men off against each other.

'*God*, he was a bastard,' Frank said.

I couldn't help smiling, partly at Frank's language, but also at the way in which he had succeeded in making himself the subject of the conversation. You could ask Frank any question and it would invariably lead to one of a handful of riffs and rants that now defined his life for him. Still, he had told me something I didn't know: in the late Fifties, not long after I was born, my grandmother and two of my uncles were inmates of the same mental home – and then there was my mother, Wendy, with her so-called 'high spirits'… Dad must have wondered what sort of family he had married into.

With a heavy sigh, Frank levered himself out of the car. I followed him through the gate and up to the front door, then watched as he jabbed at the bell with his finger. The woman who answered was bulky around the middle, as if she had a pillow strapped on beneath her clothes.

'We've come to see Joe Gausden.' Frank spoke fatalistically, like somebody expecting to be turned away. The woman stood back and signalled towards a door on the left side of the hall. 'He's in there.'

Frank led me into the front room. 'This is your nephew, Rupert,' he announced.

On the far side of the room, next to a modest fireplace, sat a man in an ankle-length cream-coloured djellaba and a pale-yellow *kufi* skullcap. He had an olive complexion and dark eyes, and both hands were clasped on a cane that stood upright between his sandalled feet. A greying beard reached down over his chest. He was fifty-eight, but looked a decade older. The word 'ayatollah' floated into my mind.

'This is Rupert,' Frank said. 'Wendy's son.'

I crossed to where Joe was sitting. He made no attempt to get to his feet. Instead, he held out his right hand, which I took in mine. Up close, his eyes had a sombre, penetrating quality; I could see no humour there. The two brothers didn't touch, I noticed, or even greet each other.

Now I was over by the fireplace I saw that Joe was not alone in the room. Against the opposite wall were four or five other men, all seated on ramshackle chairs. The way in which they were arranged, in a loose semicircle and at some distance from Joe, suggested not just that the residents of Penndale Lodge had divided into two camps, but that Joe was viewed as a performer, as entertainment.

I said hello, then took a seat facing my uncle. Frank sat to my right, with his back to the other men. I could see them beyond him, eyeing us with a kind of patient cunning.

Frank held out the two brown-paper bags. 'I bought a few things for you, Joe. I thought you might like them.'

Joe thrust his cane aside, then roughly took the bags. He opened one and peered inside. 'Are they halal?'

Frank's face assumed a look of agony. 'I don't know, Joe. No, I don't think—'

'Then what did you bring them for, you stupid bugger? They're no bloody use to me.' Joe almost slung the paper bags at Frank.

'Halal,' one of the men muttered, and winked at me.

In a voice that had lifted half an octave, Frank was defending himself. He hadn't noticed, he was saying. He didn't *know*. How was he *supposed* to know? He'd driven all the way from Four Oaks, just so Joe could meet his nephew. He'd seen an Islamic shop and bought some things he thought—

Joe didn't appear to be listening. I had the impression he had heard it all before and found it utterly contemptible. Sometimes his eyes would drift towards the bay window, but he seemed indifferent to the world outside. Sometimes, too, he glanced at me, but with such impassivity that I was rendered speechless, almost inanimate. In the end, he fixed his gaze on Frank again. Though he wasn't paying the slightest attention to what Frank was saying, he clearly derived a certain vengeful pleasure from watching his older brother squirm.

'If that's all you're capable of,' he said at last, 'you shouldn't bother coming. If that's all the *respect* you can show.'

'Oh, don't be like that, Joe…'

Later, he decided to concentrate on me. He said he could see a family resemblance. There was something of Wendy, he thought. I told him people usually said I looked more like my father. He shrugged. Either he didn't remember my father or else he just wasn't interested.

To my right, I was aware of the old men shifting on their chairs. They sucked their teeth. Dropped ash on their cardigans.

'Apparently, Wendy was frightened of you,' I said.

'Who told you that?'

'It must have been my dad.'

Joe's eyes gleamed and I felt my words had pleased him. He wasn't about to speculate on why somebody might find him frightening. What other people thought was their own affair; it had nothing to do with him. But I was struck by the fact that he seemed flattered by what I'd said. He was a vain man, even if his vanity took a decidedly unusual form. Despite that, I found I wanted him to like me.

'You haven't offered your guests any tea, Cedric,' one of the men said. My uncle's head lifted sharply and he glared across the room. 'My name's not Cedric.'

'Come on, Cedric,' another man said, nudging his neighbour. 'You don't have to be like that.'

'Call me by my proper name,' Joe thundered, 'or keep your stupid mouths shut.'

'That *is* your proper name,' the first man said.

'My *name* is Abdul Rauf. How many times do I have to tell you?'

The old men exchanged glances. One was smirking. Another choked on his tea.

Joe raised an arm and pointed across the room at them. 'You're going to bloody burn in hell, the lot of you,' he shouted. 'You're all damned.'

'That's not very nice—'

'That's rude, that is—'

'No need to lose your rag, Ced—'

'You ignorant fucking halfwits. You're all going too burn, you hear me?' Joe's voice was shaking with rage.

I looked at Frank. His head was tilted back and he had closed his eyes. Of all the people in the room, he seemed to be suffering the most.

During the hour I spent in Penndale Lodge, Joe had two such outbursts, both provoked by personal affronts. The old men were going to burn in hell, not because they were Christians, or godless, but because they refused to take Joe seriously. Their sin was mockery – a lack of deference. Somehow, though, I couldn't help feeling Joe had brought this on himself. People didn't see him as a Muslim. He was just somebody who had taken dressing-up a bit too far. He had turned himself into a spectacle – a freak; he had invited ridicule. Why had he converted to Islam? Was it a matter of genuine faith, or was it an intellectual decision, born out of his lifelong interest in comparative religion? Had he simply adopted a set of values and beliefs that would allow him to rail against a world into which he didn't seem to fit? Or could it have been a calculated attempt to upset the family, to 'stick two fingers up to the lot of us', as Frank had put it once?

I no longer recall what Joe and I said to each other after that. I only remember his physical appearance – the large, elegant hands with their prominent knuckles and blue-black veins; the beard, which was of biblical proportions; and his eyes, such a dark shade of brown that the pupils and irises were hard to tell apart. I said goodbye, knowing I might never see him again. Had I asked the right questions? Probably not. It had been difficult with all those old men listening – but perhaps it would have been difficult anyway. Joe wasn't exactly forthcoming; one would have had to pick him like a particularly stubborn lock.

What saddened me as I walked to the car was the thought that he would go on sitting in that front room, day after day, the other residents ranged against him like a Greek chorus, or a jury, or a crowd of hecklers at a comedy club. Intentionally or not, he had contrived a kind of purgatory for himself.

Driving back to Four Oaks, Frank returned to his theme, and it echoed some of what I had been thinking.

'He wouldn't play the game, you see. Just *wouldn't play the game.* He was *buggered* if he was going to do what other people wanted. He thought he was above all that. But he wasn't. He wasn't above it.'

I remembered Frank telling me how Joe behaved on the football pitch at school. Joe would have been eight or nine at the time. When the ball bounced towards him, he simply folded his arms and watched it roll past. Everyone on the touchline was shouting, *Come on, Gausden. Kick it.* But he wouldn't. A goal was scored as a result. The game was lost. He wouldn't even take part, let alone compete.

'He always had to do things his own way,' Frank said, 'and look what happened.'

'He's pretty hard on you,' I said.

'All I ever did was try and help him get back on his feet. The number of times I did that! *God!*'

'Maybe he didn't want to be helped. Maybe you should have left him alone.'

'He was still part of the family…'

Frank had missed the point. I was wondering how Joe would have reacted if Frank had called his bluff. *You want to have nothing to do with us? You want us to leave you alone? All right. We will.* But it was too late now.

Back on the dual carriageway, Frank switched lanes without signalling and the driver of the car behind us had to swerve. He gave us a loud blast on his horn.

'*Now* what?' Frank said.

Uncle Joe died in September 1988, barely two years after my one and only meeting with him. I was living in Los Angeles at the time, but Frank sent me Xeroxes of the pen-and-ink pictures his cousin Beth had drawn after the funeral. They showed Joe in a coffin, surrounded by a horde of bearded men in baggy trousers and sandals.

On my return to England, I learned that Joe's funeral had taken place in a cemetery in Walsall, and that he had been carried to his grave by members of the mosque where he had worshipped. Miriam and Beth were the only women to attend. Since Islamic law demanded that they remove their shoes, they had to stand on the wet grass in their stockinged feet. Frank was asked if he would like to say a few words. He declined. Though Joe was his brother, Frank felt marginal, excluded – a bystander rather than a true participant. According to Beth, Joe was lying on his side in the open air. His coffin, she said, was made out of fruit crates. He looked pale, unusually so, but she was able to recognize him by the slight indentation in the tip of his nose. Though the sky was overcast that day, a shaft of sunlight angled down on to Joe's face, and this was thought to be a good sign.

When I next spoke to Frank, he told me that the chapel at Tonbridge had burned down within hours of Joe's death and that he believed this was Joe's doing. Joe had taken his revenge on the school that expelled him.

'Well, it's certainly in character,' I said.

I was thinking of the army hut that had gone up in flames in Korea, but I also knew that Joe had been thrown out of his digs in Tamworth for regularly setting fire to the contents of his waste-paper basket. And then there were his various tirades against the residents of Penndale

Lodge. *You're going to burn in hell, the lot of you.*

Some years later, in the mid-Nineties, I had the idea of basing a novel on Joe's life, but my grasp on his story was sketchy at best, and I drove up to Frank and Miriam's house to see whether they could fill in any of the blanks. As usual, Frank dodged certain questions and dredged up anecdotes I had heard before, and occasionally, if pressed, he would shriek, 'I *don't know* – I *can't remember.*' It occurred to me that he might be jealous of my interest in his brother – why couldn't I show more interest in *him?* – and, feeling chastened, I sat in the kitchen and asked about his Japanese childhood, his wartime experiences and his struggles at the mill.

Not long before I left, and quite unexpectedly, he handed me an A4 envelope containing photocopies of two letters Joe had sent from South America. 'Well,' he said, looking away from me, 'you wanted to know what he was like…'

Written on headed airmail paper and dated February 18, 1951, the first letter was more than forty pages long. Joe's handwriting tilted forwards in a hurried scrawl, and there were places where the ink had smudged; I could sense the humidity, his pen gripped in fingers that were slippery with sweat. When Joe landed in Colombia to take up his job with the London Bank of South America, he had felt, he said, 'like someone who'd been away for a long time and had finally come back'.

I put the letter down, startled by what I'd just read. I had felt exactly the same when I arrived in Italy in 1982. I had given up everything – my job, my flat – and I was going to write. After driving down through France, I spent the night in a small white hotel on a rocky promontory a few miles west of Cannes – a miracle that it was open; everywhere else had closed for the winter – and when I crossed the border at Ventimiglia the next morning, my heart seemed to expand. I hadn't expected such a rush of happiness. The empty autostrada, the glitter of the Mediterranean off to the right and far below. My first Italian service station, where I stood at a zinc counter and drank a cappuccino. It felt like a homecoming. Home isn't the place you grow up in, or the place where your parents live. Home is a place you come across by chance, if you're lucky.

I picked up Joe's letter again. 'Sounds odd, doesn't it,' he had written, 'but that's the way it was.' No, Joe, I thought, not odd at all. I could see him stepping off the plane, the night so lush and muggy that it seemed to wrap its arms around him. Downtown Bogotá. The Green Room at the Hotel Granada. The Copacabana Club. Girls deliberately brushing against him as they passed him in the street. Flashed glances. The looseness of everything. This is it, he must have thought. This is it – forever.

Within a few weeks, he had assembled 'a wonderful set of friends and companions', all of them Colombian. He claimed they loved and respected him more than any Englishman they had ever come across, and that they accepted him as one of their own, not just because he spoke the language fluently, but because he willingly adopted many of their attitudes and customs. He also happened to have a naturally dark complexion. His mother, Pim, had always referred to him, affectionately, as 'little black Joe', and Joe himself, in his letters to Frank, hypothesized that there must be Latin blood in the family, 'which has come out particularly in me personally'.

Smiling, I remembered how Frank had once told me, with great relish, that we were partly descended from the Aborigines. Granny Ellis – my great-grandmother – was half Aborigine, he had assured me, being the love child of an illicit and scandalous union between an Ellis woman and an Aboriginal man. But there was also Beth's startling revelation, on a recent visit, that Frank's grandfather had been 'a black man'. She had seen a photograph of him, she said, and he was 'distinctly very, *very* dark'. Most telling for Beth was the fact that Frank had been unable – or unwilling – to trace the family on his father's side, whereas on his mother's side, apparently, he'd got all the way back to John of Gaunt.

Whatever the reason for Joe's skin colour, people in Bogotá were always mistaking him for a local. He described how an American woman had approached him at the club. 'How is it,' she asked, 'that your English is so good?' According to Joe, his reply – 'I *am* English' –

was delivered with a caustic edge, but I suspected that he found that kind of misapprehension flattering.

There were three other Englishmen at the bank who were in their twenties, but they steadfastly refused to mix with Colombians outside the office. 'Poor things!' Joe wrote. 'How much they missed!' His father, James Gausden, had spent more than thirty years in the Far East, and James – or 'Gentleman Jim', as he was known – had made a point of immersing himself in Japanese culture and tradition. Joe, too, plunged headlong into his new environment, but unlike his father he had a reckless streak and a profound disdain for convention. In expatriate society, such behaviour could be dangerous, a fact of which he was not unaware. 'If any little bit of scandal gets around or in the papers,' he wrote, 'the man is ruined – quite literally ruined.'

While dining at his boarding house, Joe met a Colombian from 'a very good family'. A few days later, he ran into the man again, on Avenida de la República, and the man invited him to the house of a friend who lived nearby. They drank superior rum, and the man's friend played the piano and sang opera and popular Spanish and Colombian songs. He also had a number of female companions who were considered 'reliable'. Joe became a regular visitor to this lavish Spanish-colonial-style house. There would be eating, drinking, dancing *amasisado* – or 'belly-to-belly,' as he explained, 'with the leg of the man between the legs of the woman' – and later there would be sex.

The men introduced him to several acquaintances of theirs, two of whom lived in the upper fringes of the city, beneath the mountains. In their atmospheric apartment, with its dark, heavily furnished rooms, they showed him albums filled with pictures of half-naked girls, all of whom were readily available. The parties would continue on into the small hours – Joe would often stay the night and turn up at the bank the following day without having gone home at all – but since everything was happening in exclusive neighbourhoods and behind closed doors, his reputation remained intact.

And then, as Joe put it, he 'got into a jam with a tart'. Shortly after arriving in Bogotá, he had picked up a girl near the Calle Real, not knowing she had served prison sentences for blackmail, drugs, and theft. Almost a year later, he had the misfortune to run into her again on his way to work. From then on, the girl began to accost him outside the bank. She told him, among other things, that she'd had a child, and that he was the father. He bribed her to stay away, but the matter had already come to the attention of his superiors. Before reassigning him to a more obscure branch of the bank in Guayaquil, the manager gave Joe a lecture about his conduct. 'I laughed openly,' Joe wrote, 'right in his face.' Joe had lost interest in his job, and had sorely tried the patience of his employers, upon whose good will he was dependent, and yet, at the same time, he was telling Frank that he wanted to settle in South America and that he didn't have the slightest intention of returning home.

Both the letters Frank had photocopied for me had been posted in Guayaquil – after Joe's demotion, in other words. In this remote, unsophisticated city, Joe had far less opportunity to indulge his vices, and deeply regretted his removal from Bogotá, where life had been such an endless round of pleasure. Apart from the Phoenix Club and the Hotel Crillon, there was nowhere to go, and before too long he found himself drawn to the red-light district, which even he admitted was 'extremely sordid'. As a precaution, he adopted a Spanish name, posing as an unemployed Colombian, but somebody saw through him and once again he was caught up in a web of intrigue and blackmail.

Within a month, he was arrested and charged with offences so 'vile and shameful' that he couldn't bring himself to go into any detail, not even with his brother. Rather than pay off the two detectives who appeared at his hotel, he insisted they escort him to the bank, where his superiors were eventually able to sort the matter out with the chief of police. 'The boss was furious,' Joe wrote, 'and said that if I was ever involved in any kind of scandal again, whether I was innocent or not, I would be thrown out of the bank on the spot and sent back to England.'

Which is precisely what happened, of course.

Within a year of writing the letters, Joe was deported from South America. He claimed the charges that had been brought against him were fabrications – 'the most filthy calumnies' – but as he himself had already pointed out, the whole question of innocence had become irrelevant. Since Frank was vague on the subject – he either couldn't, or wouldn't, tell me the full story – it was hard to know what to believe, but it seemed Joe had been cooperating with, or even orchestrating, his destiny from the very beginning, and I imagined his downfall had more to do with a long history of rebellious behaviour than with any one particular event.

I pictured him on the flight back to England, staring through the window as the plane banked to the north-east, the continent he had fallen in love with seeming for a few moments to move closer, to press itself against him, a last slow dance, but his one-line reference from the bank would have been in his pocket all the while, like a millstone. Like a death sentence. Did he realize that he had wasted the best chance he would ever be given? Did he sense that the odds were now stacked against him?

'It was a terrible blow,' Frank said of his brother's deportation. 'He was very upset by it and shaken. Very bitter. He never recovered, really.'

From that point on, Joe contrived an ever-tightening cage for himself. He sold his comfortable house in Birmingham and bought one that was smaller. Then he swapped the smaller house for something smaller still. He moved into digs by the railway arches in Tamworth. There were dead-end jobs. Months of living rough. A two-up two-down in Whitmore Reans, the poorest part of Wolverhampton. That threadbare, smoke-filled lounge in Penndale Lodge. A coffin made of fruit crates on the side of a hill. I still had so many questions, and wished I had put them to him when I'd had the opportunity. But you don't, do you? It's only when people have died that you realize what you wanted to know. Only when they cannot answer.

Years later, while staying with Frank and Miriam, I happened to mention Joe's funeral. 'It was completely foreign,' Miriam told me. 'More like Baghdad than Birmingham.'

That same weekend, thinking of visiting the grave, I asked Frank where Joe was buried. He could no longer remember. ∎

AIRSHIPS

Javier Marías

Translated by Margaret Jull Costa

A few years ago, I wrote an article in which I confessed, in rather jocular fashion, to a fear of flying, even though – with no little show of courage – I board a plane about twenty times a year. I'm pleased to say that I now feel much more confident during flights, perhaps because I've grown used to it or perhaps, as the trail of years behind us grows, we become more scornful about our possible future life and more satisfied with the life we've already accumulated. However, over a period of at least twenty years, plane journeys – of fifty minutes, two, seven or even twelve hours – could be relied upon to transform me into a highly superstitious little boy, who reached his various destinations feeling utterly drained after the hours of tension and the indescribable effort of having to 'carry' the plane.

What I've always found so odd about my fear – although it might also be the explanation – is that I first flew in a plane when I was only one month old, in the days when, for most people, flying was still a rare experience. I was born in Madrid on September 20, 1951 and on that very date – it had been planned beforehand, so it wasn't that he took one look at me and fled – my father set off on the first of his Atlantic crossings and travelled to America with a contract to teach at Wellesley College, Massachusetts – a college for young ladies – for the academic year of 1951–2. My mother followed a month later, taking with her my two older brothers, Miguel and Fernando, as well as me, the newborn baby. I don't know what the travelling conditions were like (apart from the fact that I was dressed all in pink, because they had been expecting a girl), or whether I cried a little or a lot as we crossed the ocean, or whether the crew members of Iberia or TWA made a fuss of me or loathed me. And I recall nothing, either, of the return journey – NewYork–Madrid – nine or ten months later. I do, however, have a vague recollection of my third trip by plane. I was just four years old, had acquired another brother, Álvaro, and my father had decided to take us all to New Haven, Connecticut, at the behest of Yale University. It's not a very pleasant memory: I can see myself – not crying, but very, very angry – lying in the aisle, refusing to get up and doubtless obstructing crew and passengers alike. I don't know how long the tantrum lasted – possibly a couple of minutes, possibly much longer – but I'm sure that if, as an adult, I had seen the child that was me, I would have hated him for blocking the aisle; more than that, I would have thought it a bad omen, which is always rather worrying in mid-flight.

It's probably a well-known fact – although I can't be sure because people don't talk about it much – that those of us who suffer in planes tend to invest a great deal of feverish, exhausting mental activity in our role as, how can I put it, 'imaginary co-pilots'. As I said, my fear of flying is now abating, but throughout my life I've spent many hours on board in a state of permanent alertness, attentive not only to any possible changes of mood in the engines, or to the plane's recognizable or unexpected noises, or to its scheduled or unscheduled ups and downs, but also to everything else around me, in particular the air hostesses and the stewards and even the captain's variable tones of voice over the intercom – whether he sounds calm or nervous.

I have tended to see 'signs' or 'premonitions' in the tiniest details and, given that all superstitions are arbitrary, it always used to make me feel uneasy if a passenger stood talking in the aisle for too long, especially if he or she was Japanese, don't ask me why. Nor was I soothed, particularly on long-haul flights, by the sight of other excessively relaxed and uninhibited passengers who, far from keeping a close eye on our flight path, as is the duty of all caring and committed travellers, laughed and drank, moved around the cabin, played cards or performed other equally grave and reckless acts, or so it seemed to me. In short, I spend, or have spent, the entire journey 'controlling' and 'helping' and 'protecting' the whole hazardous crossing with my tireless thoughts. A four-year-old child blocking the aisle would definitely have strained my nerves. I'm not sure I would have been able to refrain from giving him a good slap.

No, I would doubtless have contained my irritation because since I reached the age of shaving, I've always behaved myself on board planes, unlike the callow creature I was then. I have limited myself to keeping a firm grip on an open newspaper (of the broadsheet variety, so that there's no chance of my sneaking a glance out of the windows), either pretending to read it or actually reading it – although without taking in a single word – meanwhile fending off any attempts at conversation (one doesn't want to become distracted and neglect one's duty as lookout), demolishing at high speed whatever food is placed in front of me, and all the while clutching some wooden object I've brought with me for the purpose, since there doesn't tend to be any wood – a major oversight – on those flying submarines.

It was a similar remark, made in that earlier article, and my subsequent confession that I'd worn out the wooden toothpicks and matches I grasped between my fingers, that provoked a charming Iberia air hostess into sending me a letter and a little wooden key ring in the form of a plane, so that, in future, I wouldn't have to make a fool of myself abroad, holding those grubby matches and toothpicks. And that same air hostess, as well as recounting a few anecdotes from her long experience in the air, made me think of planes, for the first time, as relatively 'humanizable' objects, which one could, in a way, and depending on the circumstances, mentally direct. Not that there's anything very remarkable about that. Indeed, it's perfectly normal. She told me in her letter that whenever the plane she was on lurched or bumped about a bit or jolted, she would issue a silent order: 'Down, boy!' Yes, an order, an exorcism, a persuasive word.

In *The Mirror of the Sea* – a magnificent book I translated into Spanish several years ago now – the great Polish-English novelist Joseph Conrad speaks of ships having their own character and spirit, their own norms of behaviour, their caprices, rebellions and gratitudes. Of how, in large measure, their performance and reliability depend on the treatment they receive from captain and crew.

If treated with respect, affection, consideration, care and tact, a ship, says Conrad, is grateful and responds by trying hard and giving of its best (or, rather, her best, since curiously and significantly almost the only objects that merit a gender in the English language are ships, which are always referred to as 'she' and not, as would be more natural, as 'it'). If, on the contrary, the relationship between them is one of superiority, disdain or is simply too demanding, authoritarian or neglectful, abusive, inconsiderate or even despotic, ships react badly, and feel no 'loyalty' and fail to 'protect' their crews at moments of risk or danger.

Ships, writes Conrad, are 'not exactly what men make them. They have their own nature; they can of themselves minister to our self-esteem by the demand their qualities make upon our skill and their shortcomings upon our hardiness and endurance.' Further on, he adds:

> The love that is given to ships is profoundly different from the love men feel for every other work of their hands – the love they bear to their houses, for instance – because it is untainted by the pride of possession. The pride of skill, the pride of responsibility, the pride of endurance there may be, but otherwise it is a disinterested sentiment. No seaman ever cherished a ship, even if she belonged to him, merely because of the profit she put in his pocket. No one, I think, ever did; for a ship-owner, even of the best, has always been outside the pale of that sentiment embracing in a feeling of intimate,

equal fellowship the ship and the man, backing each other against the implacable, if sometimes dissembled, hostility of their world of waters.

Later still, Conrad describes the touching words, tantamount to a funeral oration, uttered by the captain of a brig that had sunk:

'No ship could have done so well… She was small, but she was good. I had no anxiety. She was strong. Last voyage I had my wife and two children in her. No other ship could have stood so long the weather she had to live through for days and days before we got dismasted a fortnight ago. She was fairly worn out, and that's all. You may believe me. She lasted under us for days and days, but she could not last for ever. It was long enough. I am glad it is over. No better ship was ever left to sink at sea on such a day as this.'

Conrad sums up by saying: 'She had lived, he had loved her; she had suffered, and he was glad she was at rest.'

We air passengers are not accustomed to perceiving, or even imagining, planes in this way, as almost animate beings, with a capacity for suffering and endurance, requiring consideration and esteem, and being sensitive, almost, to gratitude and rancour. We board them and can barely distinguish between them; we know nothing of their age or their past history; we don't even notice their names, which, in Spain at least, are chosen in such a bureaucratic, pious spirit, so lacking in poetry, adventure and imagination, that they're hard to retain and recognize if ever we entrust ourselves to them again. I would like to ask Iberia, in this the twenty-first century, to abandon their anodyne patriotic gestures and adulatory nods to the Catholic Church – all those planes called *Our Lady of the Pillar* and *Our Lady of Good Remedy*, *The City of Burgos* and *The City of Tarragona* – and instead choose names that are more cheerful and more literary. I, for one, would feel safer and more reassured, more protected, if I knew I was flying in the *The Red Eagle* or *The Fire Arrow* or even *Achilles* or *Emma Bovary* or *Falstaff* or *Liberty Valance* or *Nostromo*.

Perhaps reading that air hostess's epistolary revelations had something to do with the diminution of my fear. Until that comment of hers it had never occurred to me that captains might have a similar relationship with their planes as old seadogs do with their ships, and that air crews are like sailors. Perhaps the things that surprised and disturbed me during my long watches as a fearful traveller – a murmur, a squeak, a bump, a lurch – were perfectly recognizable to them, familiar, customary, the reactions of each individualized and distinguishable plane, just as we recognize the people close to us by their gestures and intonations, their silences and vacillations, so much so that, often, we don't even need them to speak to know what's wrong, what's going through their minds, what they're suffering or worrying about or plotting or waiting for.

This possibility soothes me. We live in an age that tends to depersonalize even people and is, in principle, averse to anthropomorphism. Indeed, such a tendency is often criticized, erroneously and foolishly in my view, since that 'rapprochement' between the human and the non-human is quite natural and spontaneous, and far from being an attempt to deprive animals, plants and objects of their respective selves, it places them in the category of the 'humanizable', which is, for us, the highest and most respectable of categories.

I know people who talk to, question, spoil, threaten or even quarrel with their computers, saying things like: 'Right now, you behave yourself,' or thanking them for their help. There's nothing wrong with that, it's perfectly understandable. In fact, given how often we travel in planes, the odd thing about our relationship with them – those complex machines endowed with movement to which we surrender ourselves and that transport us through the air – is that it isn't more 'personal', or more 'animal', or more 'sailor-like', if you prefer. Perhaps those who crew them haven't known how to communicate this to us. I've never seen them pat a plane, as you might pat a horse to calm or reward it; I've never seen planes being groomed and cleaned and tidied, except very hurriedly and impatiently; I've never seen them loved as Conrad's captain loved his sunken brig; I've never seen air hostesses – who spend a lot of time on-board – treat them with the respect and care, at once fatherly and comradely, enjoyed by ships.

That's what I would like to see, less cool efficiency and more affection, and I'm sure that I, along with many other tense, vigilant passengers, would become infected by their confidence and be able to relax, because then planes, like ships in the old days, would have their 'reputation', and we would know something of their voyages, their history, their deeds, their past and their future. The pilots, instead of frightening us with their usual litany of cold, hair-raising facts ('We will be flying at an absurdly high altitude, the temperature outside is unbelievably cold, etc.'), could say: 'This plane, the *Pierre Ménard*, has had an amazing life so far. It was born ten years ago, has made five hundred flights and crossed the Atlantic on sixty-three previous occasions. It has always responded well to us, even in the most unfavourable of circumstances. It's a docile plane by nature, but very sensitive as well. Why, I remember once…'

Well, I leave the rest up to the airlines. Perhaps it isn't too much to ask for a little more literature or – which comes to the same thing – a little uniqueness; a little history and background; a little life. ∎

THE MIND-CHILD

Remembering J.G. Ballard

Will Self

Jim had been in hospital over Christmas – the chemical refinery of the Hammersmith, which faces out over the *veldt-in-urbe* of Wormwood Scrubs – and the experience had nearly done for him. 'They were suggesting he move to a single room at the end of the ward,' said Claire, his girlfriend, 'and you know what that means.' Of course I did: ninety per cent of the spending on healthcare in any given English individual's life takes place in their last six weeks. Up until then welfare provision may have been patchy, but a citizen's final demise is invariably full-board and en suite – assuming, that is, express checkout.

Claire extracted Jim from the hospital and took him back to her flat in Shepherd's Bush. I could picture the rhythms of this phase of their life together, the coming and going of the district nurse, the pitter-patter of tiny pills. When I spoke to Claire on the phone she remained simply delighted to have got him back from the clutches of hospital medicine – with its all too often pointless heroism – and restored to a domestic context. Ballard, the most outlandish of fictional imaginers, had always dug out his wellspring by the hearth, and remained the

J.G. Ballard, London, 1991

perfect exemplar of Magritte's dictum: a bourgeois in his life, a revolutionary in his dreams.

Claire worked at her computer during the days, a baby alarm next to her mouse mat so she could hear if he needed anything; then, when it was time to go to bed she took it with her. 'When I take it upstairs,' she wrote to me, 'it's as if I'm carrying his breathing self in the little plastic machine. I hold it very carefully in my hand, like a precious living thing... (I haven't told him).' I found this quite unbearably affecting; indeed, I had become involved in all of this in a way I found both difficult to understand – and painfully obvious.

I had propped a copy of Jim's memoir *Miracles of Life* up on the bookcase in the kitchen, so that each morning, on coming downstairs, I was met by the image of the child Ballard riding his tricycle in Shanghai. I felt myself opening out to the numinous in my communion with the dying writer, an intimation of alternative realities, including, perhaps, some in which we had been as close emotionally – and physically – as we had been imaginatively; for to pretend to an intimate relationship with Jim would've been presumptuous – we had met at most five or six times.

The first had been in 1994, when Ballard was publishing *Rushing to Paradise*, his warped eco-parable version of *The Tempest*, wherein Greenpeace activists and South Seas sybarites run amok on an atoll used for nuclear weapons testing. Like so many before me, I had made the pilgrimage to the Surrey dormitory town of Shepperton to interview its sage for a newspaper. All was as has been described in scores of articles: the neat little semi along the somnolent suburban street, the mutant yucca straining against the mullions of the front window, the Ford Granada humped in the driveway. Inside, the small rooms were dominated by the reproductions of lost Paul Delvaux nudes that Jim had commissioned himself. Other than this oddity the decor was an exercise in unconcern – and not a studied one.

'Would you like a drink?' he asked, vigorous in an open-necked white shirt. 'I've got everything.'

I had had, of course, a fantasy of quaffing Scotch with Ballard – I knew of his legendary and unashamed consumption: the first tumbler poured in the morning when he returned from the school run, the leisurely topping-up throughout the writing day, two fingers per hour, clackety-clack, as he typed his way into inner space. However, like a lot of alcoholics, I couldn't risk taking a drink in the afternoon, especially if I was working: the comedown was instant, I would have to have more – and more; no leisurely sousing but a sudden spirituous downpour, so I asked, 'Can I have a cup of tea?'

Jim grimaced. 'Too much trouble, boiling water and things…' He gestured vaguely.

I settled for water. We sat down in the back sitting room, looking out through French windows to a sunlit garden. Jim chortled. 'So, you've managed to extricate yourself from that cocaine-smuggling business, have you?'

He was referring to a recent bust I'd had for possessing hashish in the Orkney Islands, where I'd been living up until a couple of months previously – the case had recently been heard at the Sheriff Court in Kirkwall, and made a few column inches down south. I explained the situation, but he seemed utterly uninterested in the detail: possession/supply, hash/coke – it was, his manner suggested, all one to him. I found myself strangely bothered by how dégagé Ballard was, as if it should be his responsibility to either condemn or condone my actions. It was absurd: true, he was thirty-one years my senior, but I was a grown man. Besides, he wasn't my father; or, at least, not biologically.

For that was the problem: as well as the abiding infantilism of my own malaise – the need to blame everyone else for my own derelictions, my ethical clumsiness and emotional incontinence – I also believed I was Ballard's mind-child, that my hypertrophied creative impulse had burst from his domed forehead, slathering his remaining greyish hair with amniotic fluid. It's a sensitive business, this one of literary patrimony – although I'd never had any anxiety about my influences. There were those writers whose work spoke to me; those whose mannerisms, tropes, accidents of style were – in Auden's memorable acronym – GETS, 'Good Enough to Steal'; and then there were a very select few who had carved out the conceptual space within which I sought to stake my own claim. Of these, Ballard was the pre-eminent.

The great wind from nowhere of October 1987: I awoke in a sepia dawn to a cacophony of tortured metal; through the slats of my venetian blind I could see that six-by-three-foot panels of corrugated iron were being torn from the scaffolding on the old LCC council block opposite. The blasts were strong enough to be holding some of them upright and pushing them along the road surface, striking sparks. Nature, kept away from the city by its mighty radiation – repelled by roofs, walls and fences – had broken through. Except that in this mundane urban context the wind – no matter how strong – could not possibly be from nowhere, only a little further north, say Camden Town.

I associate my Ballardian apprenticeship with this period, in my middle twenties, when, recently sprung from four months in rehab, I shared a flat on Barnsbury Road in Islington with an elfin would-be mime artist. We painted the floors red and listened to southern soul on an antiquated valve record player; occasionally my flatmate did a handspring – a manoeuvre he had used to evade the bulls in Pamplona.

I was nervy and racked by caffeine and nicotine – one morning I even *overdosed* on coffee, no mean achievement. I had a writerly girlfriend who was more advanced than me – she'd actually completed a novel, and in due course it was published. I found it difficult to get *at* her: after sweaty midnights, then throughout those cold dawns I struggled to prise apart her thin and resistant white limbs. I recall the feel of hand-me-down parental linen – and sinking into the trough of a broken-backed bed dragged back from the furniture warehouse on Liverpool Road. She turned away from my carefully crafted caresses and I saw peculiar spiral markings on her bare back and stubby neck.

Ringworm. We both had it – the vermiculation of our short-let accommodation had bored through the plaster and into our flesh.

For a vermifuge we read *Crash*, and savoured its opening lines: 'Vaughan died yesterday in his last car-crash. During our friendship he had rehearsed his death in many crashes, but this was his only true accident.' This said it all: the intersection between the performative and the desperate; the gargantuan alienation of the modern machine/man matrix trumped by a studied act of self-violence. When we were out, driving in her Renault 5 van, she would grab hold of my arm, yanking the steering wheel. 'Crash!' she'd exhale in my ear. 'Crash!' I'd breathe back – and this was the best consummation we ever managed, except for one cold afternoon coupling in the back of the van.

We had driven out from London to the Isle of Grain in the Thames estuary. Since an epiphany experienced the previous summer on a sunlit street in Mayfair, I had spent more and more time cruising the periphery of London: how was it that I had never visited – nor even envisaged – the mouth of the river that ran through my natal city? And so I was drawn to those desolate places where redundant heavy industry was sinking into the mire between retail barns and business parks: Erith Marsh, Thamesmead, Tilbury – and eventually the Ultima Thule of Grain itself, where the cracked pavements were sutured with weeds and the rust-streaked pipelines of the oil refinery snaked through the marsh grasses. The necrotic flesh of plastic bags flapped on barbed-wire fences, crows descended on the corpse of a muddy field; seagulls followed the plough, pylons engaged in a tug of war with high-tension cables, and the cloud piled up over Sheppey, black upon grey. In the dully humbling cul-de-sac of the last council estate in southern England a child's bicycle lay unclaimed on an unmown verge; beyond the concrete baffler of the sea wall the Maunsell Towers Sea Forts strode towards the horizon, like Wells's Martian tripods.

On these forays into the interzones I took photographs and made cryptic notes that no one – not even me – would ever read again. I felt myself to be engaged in some crucial project: the discovery of an essential reality that remained inviolate, incapable of being assimilated to the marketable portions of locale and territory into which the land was being divided. This was no village England or rural idyll, nor could it be incorporated into the smoothly functioning machinery of the conurbation, where built environment, transportation and humanity all played their part in the Taylorization of space.

On the muddy foreshore below the village of Grain there were cracked dragon's teeth, and an old stone causeway, greasy-green with seaweed, that led out to Grain Tower, a Second World War gun emplacement. I piloted the Renault along the rough track beneath an embankment that protected the power station from the Medway. Freighters came drifting in on the tide, their superstructures as high and white and rectangular as blocks of flats. I stopped the van and – terribly aroused – made my slinky moves.

That brisk March day the sex was probably no great shakes – only the usual soft rasp and toothy snag; but the ridged metal of the van's floor, the awkward positions we had to assume in order to fit – one into the other, both into the abbreviated compartment – these were thrillingly hard correlates of the interzone that lay beyond the Renault's double doors: we were fucking the furnaces and cooling towers, the generators and coal hoppers. Our breathy spasms and cramped ejaculations reverberated against the chilled earth and the cold sky. On the way back to London we bought a cheese and pickle sandwich at a petrol station and as we shared it the yellow-white gratings dropped into our laps like the shredded skin of H-bomb victims. I had her stained underwear stuffed in the pocket of my jacket.

The relationship staggered on for another nine months; then, at the beginning of 1988, my mother arrived punctually at the terminal stages of cancer. Each day I went to her flat in Kentish Town to give her sublingual morphine sulphate and other, more cack-handed ministrations. Perhaps, facing this enormity, I was too needy – or maybe my girlfriend's neediness was now insupportable; one or the other, it was no longer enough for her to yank my arm and implore me to 'Crash!' I *was* crashing. We had read Ballard together, there had been the sex on the Isle of Grain – and that was enough: *The Atrocity*

Exhibition, Vermilion Sands, Hello America – books I had initially consumed in my early teens, when I used to guzzle up the quintuple-decker sandwiches of science fiction I carried back from East Finchley library (rubber-soled sneakers squeaking on the polished floors, the deferential hush now long since sacrificed to espresso machines and computer terminals; up on the wall an old photograph of Dame Henrietta Barnett herding sheep across the fields where Hampstead Garden Suburb now stood, but which had once been an Edwardian interzone).

Then, I had paid no particular attention to Ballard, regarding his works as of a piece with all the other dystopias I hung out in. Possibly I had noticed a certain harder edge, a smoother dovetailing between the commonplace and the fantastic; maybe the wanting seed had been planted. Whatever. But when I reread Ballard the seed germinated with nightmarish alacrity, sending shoots into every portion of my brain. I had been struggling – as every wannabe writer should – with what it was that I could conceivably write. My experience was both threadbare and mundane: the conveyor-belt smoothness of tarmac paths between green privet curtains; dysfunctional family neuroses as regularly patterned as Sanderson wallpaper; painful experimentation with drugs – teaching myself to shoot up, puncturing my skinny forearms with needles while outside the steel-framed windows pigeons coo-burbled. *The human organism is an atrocity exhibition at which he is an unwilling spectator.* All this, I knew, was nothing; my mind was a tabula rasa sullied with the smears of licked fingertips picking up granules of cocaine and amphetamine sulphate.

Before I'd gone into rehab I'd essayed a few things: a post-apocalyptic novella called *The Caring Ones*, in which the ton of diamorphine that was allegedly kept in the Mass Disaster Room in the Royal Free Hospital became the cynosure of all power struggles between the pain-ravaged survivors of the bomb. I still have the manuscript somewhere – but that says more about my obsessive need to accumulate paper than anything else, for it was crap. Utter crap. There were also a handful of comic vignettes and reams of self-indulgent diarizing of the kind that no self-respecting crafter of fiction should ever permit. I had ideas, certainly, but no means of anchoring them with authenticity.

Ballard showed the way: the fiction of the twenty-first century, the fiction that would matter, was there on the Isle of Grain, there in the interzones, there in the psyches of all of us who appreciated the three-mile sinuous chicane of the Westway flyover, there in our numbed responses to those superfluities of space and time that, together with our own narcissistic subjectivity, constituted the very essence of what Marc Augé has termed 'supermodernity'. That Ballard had got there first – and got there furthest – was only testimony to his genius. He was one of that small coterie of artists who, unafraid of the consequences, had been prepared to turn their minds over to the daemons of creation to make of them what they would. Acutely conscious that in the post-lapsarian world that followed the Holocaust and Hiroshima, no value would escape re-evaluation, Ballard had turned his back on the cosy sentimentalities of so-called naturalistic fiction, its immersion in the he-said, she-said, we-watched of interpersonality. No longer, he averred, could the novelist – like an origami deity – fix fate by folding the page.

Six years later, in Shepperton, I was a published writer – and what was far better, Ballard had read my stuff and approved. I switched on the tape recorder and we talked for a couple of hours, talked easily, ranging freely across the fictional terrain where our estates marched. There were anecdotes that Jim told, the matter of which was not unexpected: the genuine paranoia of William Burroughs, whom he had known fairly well in the 1970s; the continuing capacity of his cloistered life to confound visitors; the whisky... But overall it was a conversation about writing, and the worlds that writing actualized, and a conversation about the world, and the writings that it provoked.

The shadows crept across the pocket-handkerchief lawn; if, at the outset, I had been thinking of Jim as a putative parent, when it was time for me to go I was having difficulty not regarding him as a friend. I was heading back to town, to Soho, to meet up with Damien Hirst and his coterie ('He's really a novelist,' Jim had said, 'who writes very short books').There would be a lot of drinking, a lot of cocaine, a headlong fall into a dark night of shebeens and spielers. Did he…? I ventured to Jim…ever go out much? Would it be possible for us to meet up again?

And here, perhaps, my memory lets me down, because what I *think* Ballard said in reply was one of the most pithily instructive lessons about life and literature that I've ever been handed.True, it was a little late for me to be learning this – but then, no one had ever offered to teach me before. No, he said, he didn't go out much – and besides, there was probably too great a disparity in our ages for us to find much common social ground. Moreover, writers knowing one another in the flesh was almost entirely beside the point; the true communion existed in the texts, and we had that with each other already.

Having placed myself so overtly as a disciple, and then – quite uncharacteristically – to have risked the rebuff, I was surprised by how well I took it. As I walked back to the station it occurred to me that this was because what Ballard had said he meant, and that furthermore it was true.There could be no greater meeting of minds than the one we had already experienced amid the twisted hulks of cars abandoned en route to the terminal beach; even sexually, with his easy acceptance – on the page – of the homoerotic, I had assessed the heft of his body, apprehended the geometry of his genitals. If Ballard felt the same way about me – but a small part of it – then it remained a far more mutual relationship than any I had ever contracted for through the mere accident of propinquity.

And so I took him at his word – and kept away. A year or so later, when I heard that David Cronenberg was about to film Ballard's *Crash*, I did get in touch. It was well known among Ballardians that the novel had been optioned by several producers over the years, but was widely regarded as unfilmable. There was said to be a script in existence by the British poet Heathcote Williams. While I had no objection to Cronenberg taking on *Crash* – how could I? It wasn't mine to bestow – I nonetheless had a perverse sense of ownership: this seminal novel, with its celebration of the autoerotic potential of car crashes, was played out against a backdrop that seemed to me to be the core of contemporary London – its motorways and interzones. The climactic crashes themselves – from the narrator's initiatory collision to Vaughan's final plunge – took place along Western Avenue and on the Chiswick flyover. The car-crash cult's field of operations was the badlands in the purlieus of Heathrow Airport, the scrublands of Hillingdon and Hayes, the cavernous warehouses and hangars of its Perimeter Road, the reservoir-cratered moonscape of Staines and Shepperton itself – where Ballard's alter ego, 'James', also lives. To transpose this to Toronto would be a dreadful solecism.

I got Jim on the phone. 'No, no,' he barked in his genial RAF-officer tones. 'You don't get it at all. The whole point of *Crash* is that it could take place anywhere in the urbanized world. I absolutely relish the idea of Cronenberg filming in Toronto. It's the perfect location – so anonymous, so dreary.'

To have pursued my case for London with Jim would've been crass – but I also spoke with the director himself on the phone. Was there – I wondered – an opening for a screenwriter? Cronenberg laughed. 'No, I don't think so.' He sounded amiable – and very Canadian. 'You know I write all my shooting scripts myself.'

In the event Cronenberg's film of *Crash* was entirely acceptable. I could quibble with the casting and some of the dialogue, but the locations were indeed massively beside the point, for the director was perfectly in tune with the writer's own vision of cities reduced to the sum of their component parts: concrete, steel, tar. The ceaseless movement of the traffic on the freeway beneath the apartment where James (James Spader) and Catherine (Deborah Unger) perform their soulless acts, skin upon skin, is only the analogue of the ceaseless movement of all traffic, everywhere. The gap between one car and the next is the gap between Tokyo and Los Angeles, New York and London, Paris and Moscow, Beijing and São Paulo – conurbations that retain an allegedly safe distance from each other while hurtling around an orbital road. All this, until the fossils have been burned and entropy ensues – as Jim foresaw: the creepers wreathing the gantries at Cape Canaveral will be the organic confirmation that futurity was just a moment in time.

I stayed away from Shepperton, writing only the occasional note, or sending a book I'd published, or a bottle of Scotch I thought he might like. When my third child was born Jim sent me a letter: 'Now they outnumber you!' But of course, ever since his wife's death in 1964, he himself had been completely outnumbered. Eventually, in 2006, I returned, with the pretext of another interview. This time I came on a folding bicycle and pedalled my way down the suburban street, but otherwise everything remained the same: the somnolent semi, with the yucca in the front window now completely overgrown, a triffid that had usurped the household and perhaps demanded its own troublesome cups of tea.

I had already heard rumours that Jim was ill, but he seemed perfectly hale – intrigued by my folding bicycle and altogether welcoming. Once we were seated at the table in the front room he expostulated, 'Why don't you ever come to see me!' And the last twelve years fell away like multicoloured fish scales. I almost blurted out, 'But you told me…!' Then didn't. Instead we talked as before, yet this time – or so it seemed to me – with an easier intimacy: time does this to human lives, evening them up, so that in due course the jejune disciple becomes the well-worn near-contemporary.

Jim talked of his time in the internment camp in Shanghai and with great frankness of the horrors he had witnessed as a child. The novel that was about to be published, *Kingdom Come*, was in some ways a retread of preoccupations he had showcased in his writing going all the way back to *High Rise* (1975) – material sufficiency as a prelude to dreadful ennui, violence as an antidote to boredom, *enfin* the revolt of the bourgeoisie – but from the way he discussed his past I now realize that Jim must already have been working on the memoir *Miracles of Life*.

Two or three dinners in Shepherd's Bush followed. We ate either at the Brackenbury or Esarn Kheaw, a northern Thai restaurant. These were quietly sociable affairs – Jim and Claire, my wife, Deborah, and I. The talk was of current events, families, the patchwork of cultural interests to be expected of such representative types: writers, editors, journalists. In many ways the meetings were antithetical to the fierce communion I had experienced with Jim's psyche in the pages of his books. I had started out, in the 1970s, following him along a cramped and dangerous tunnel when he was unquestionably in the avant-garde, hacking away at the rage-resistant fabric of society, inching his way forward into conceptual space; now we sat opposite one another at a candlelit table and chatted about the London Congestion Charge. I liked both modalities equally well.

Jim had never made any secret of his diagnosis with terminal prostate cancer – he had been open in the press and frank in person. But there was, I felt, a strange disconnection between his seeming acceptance of his own death and his manner, which suggested that the valediction itself could be an eternity. First, the memoir, and now there was a second book of leave-taking in the pipeline, a series of discourses with his oncologist, Jonathan Waxman. I took this stoicism as in line with a life that in some respects had been lived backwards: the tight bomb-pattern of *thanatos* falling in the first three decades, the subsequent ones more and more vivified; and contrasted it with my own overweening neurosis, the mewling all morning over a hangnail, the adolescent hysteria that popped up to accompany the pubescent spots that still erupted on my middle-aged face. ∎

A SIGN OF
WEAKNESS

Terrence Holt

M y first call night as an intern, I ran into Dr M, one of the senior
attendings, whom I had known for several years. 'How's it
going?' he asked me. I told him I was on call. 'First call?' He smiled. 'I
remember my first call. About ten o'clock that night, my resident said
to me, "I'm going to be just behind that door. Call me if you need me.
But remember – it's a sign of weakness."'

   I don't recall my response: I don't think I even had time to consider
the story until evening, when the frantic milling about that makes up
an intern's day had started to wind down. That day, we filled up early
– three opportunistic pneumonias from the HIV clinic; a prison inmate
transferred from Raleigh with haemoptysis, presumably TB; a fever-
of-unknown-origin.

   Keith, the resident, whose job it was to direct me in my labours,
felt this was a good day – his work was essentially done by five, as
together we wrote admission orders starting the work-up of the
mysterious fever. He said to me, 'I'm heading off to read. Call me if
you need anything.'

'But it's a sign of weakness, right?' I said, remembering Dr M's story. Keith laughed. 'Right.' And sauntered off down the hall.

Later, I was on the eighth floor, getting sign-out from one of the interns on the pulmonary service. It was almost seven – this was early in the year, and nobody was getting out before dinner. This intern was post-call, red-eyed and barely making sense. Her sign-out list was eleven patients long. I don't remember any of it except the one: Mrs B was listed as a 'DNR/DNI 57yo WF w/scleroderma–>RD'.

'She's a whiner,' the intern explained. 'Don't get too excited about anything she says.' She paused. 'I mean, if she looks bad, get a gas or something, but basically she's a whiner.'

Whiner, I wrote down in the margin of the list.

I sat at the workstation for some time after that, running through lab results on the computer – the scheduled seven p.m. draw was still going on, so there was nothing new on the screen, but it calmed me to go through the exercise.

A nurse stuck her head through the door. 'Doctor?'

I was still unused to people calling me that.

'Do you know the lady in twenty-six?'

I fished the sign-out sheets out of my pocket. 'What's her name?' There were too many sheets. The nurse gave me the name and my eye fell on it at the same time. Whiner.

'What's her problem?'

'She says she's feeling short of breath.'

'Vitals?' I heard myself ask, marvelling at my tone of voice as I did. The nurse pulled a card out of her pocket and read off a series of numbers. When she was done I realized I hadn't heard any of them.

The nurse read them again. This time, I wrote them down. Then I spent a minute studying them. She was afebrile, I noted. That was good. Her heart rate was ninety-six, a high number I had no idea how to interpret. Her blood pressure was 152 over eighty-four, another highish set of numbers that told me nothing. Her respiratory rate was twenty-six – also high, and vaguely disquieting. Her O_2 sat – the oxygen content of her blood – was ninety-two per cent: low, and in the context of that high respiratory rate not a good sign. The nurse was still looking at me. 'I hear she's a whiner,' I said hopefully. The nurse shrugged. 'She asked me to call you.'

The patient was alone in a double room. The light in the room was golden, the late sun of the July evening slanting through the high window. The face that turned to me as I knelt at the bedside was curiously unwrinkled. Her skin had a stretched and polished look, her features strangely immobile, the entire effect disturbingly like a doll's face. Her chest rose and fell, but her nostrils did not flare. Her mouth was a tight puncture in the centre of her face. Only her eyes were mobile, following me as I moved.

'What seems to be the problem?' My voice had taken on a strange quality: tight, almost strangled.

'Are you my doctor?'

'I'm the doctor on call,' I explained.

'I can't breathe.'

I looked at her for a minute.

'What do you mean?'

'I can't...catch my breath.'

I thought, but nothing brilliant came to mind. 'Are you feeling dizzy?' I asked.

'No. Just. Short of breath.'

I watched, counting. They were quick, shallow breaths, about twenty-eight of them to the minute.

I bent over her and placed my stethoscope on her back. I heard air moving, in and out, and a faint, light rustling, like clothes brushing together in a darkened closet. 'I'll be right back,' I said, and left the room to find her nurse. A few minutes later the nurse reported back to me. 'Eighty-nine per cent.'

'Is she on any oxygen?' I should know this, I thought. I'd just been looking at her.

The nurse shook her head.

'Put her on two litres and check again.'

Ten minutes later the nurse was back. I was in the doctors' workroom, looking up 'scleroderma' on the Web.

'Ninety-one per cent.'

'That's better,' I said hopefully.

The nurse shook her head. 'Not on two litres. Not how hard she's working.'

'You think she's working hard?'

The nurse smiled thinly. 'Do you want to check a gas, Doctor?'

I smiled back, genuinely relieved that someone was willing to tell me what to do. 'That's a great idea,' I said. 'Can you do that?'

'No. But you can. I'll get the stuff.'

An arterial blood gas is a basic bedside procedure – the kind of thing third-year medical students are encouraged to learn. It involves sticking a needle into an artery and drawing off three or four ccs of blood. The reason a doctor has to draw it is that arteries lie deeper than veins. Even the relatively superficial radial artery – at the wrist, the one you press when checking a pulse – lies a good half-inch deep in most people, and sticking a needle in it stings more than a bit. I was not at that time very skilled at procedures – the arterial blood gas was about the limit of my expertise – but to my relief I had no trouble getting it: bright red blood flashed into the syringe. The patient bore this without a grimace, although by now I wondered if the skin on her face was capable of expression at all. Her eyes regarded the needle in her wrist.

'How are you feeling?'

'A little. Better.'

I pulled the needle out, held a pad of gauze to her wrist.

She subsided into the bed. 'But still. Short of breath.'

I watched her. Twenty-six, twenty-eight. Shallow, the muscles at her neck straining with each one.

'I'll be back in a bit,' I said, rising with the syringe in my hand. 'Call if you need anything.' But it's a sign of weakness, I echoed to myself. I hurried on down the hall, the echo following.

While I waited for the lab to process the gas. I skimmed over fifteen pages about scleroderma, a mysterious, untreatable condition in which the skin and organs stiffen. The most feared complications are cardiac and pulmonary. Some victims develop fibrosis of the heart early in the course of the disease, and quickly die, as the accumulation of gristle disrupts the heart's conduction system. In the lungs, collagen invades the membranes where the blood exchanges oxygen and carbon dioxide with air: the lungs stiffen, thicken and fail.

It is possible to get an idea of how this would feel. Putting your head in a paper bag is a dim shadow of it; thick quilts piled high come closer. The difference, of course, is that you can't throw scleroderma off. The bag stays dark; the quilts simply thicken, over years.

The blood gas was not encouraging. The numbers on the screen told me several things. Her blood was acidic. CO_2 trapped in her lungs was mixing with water in her blood to make carbonic acid. The acid was chewing up her stores of bicarbonate, which meant that her lungs were getting worse faster than her kidneys could compensate. The really bad news was the amount of oxygen dissolved in her blood, which at a partial pressure of fifty-four millimetres was unusually low, especially for someone getting supplementary O_2. Taken together, these numbers spoke of lungs that were rapidly losing access to the outside air.

I remembered a patient I had taken care of during an ER rotation a year earlier, an old lady with pneumonia. I had gotten a gas on her, too, and it had come back essentially normal. The attending had asked me to interpret it. 'It's normal,' I said. 'And?' the attending replied, directing my attention to the patient gasping on the gurney. I looked at her for a moment. She was breathing about forty times a minute. 'You're about to tube her,' I said. 'Right,' the attending said, and did just that. A normal gas on somebody working hard is a bad sign. A below-normal gas on somebody working hard to breathe on supplementary O_2 is a very bad sign, especially if her chart carries the notation 'DNI'. The letters stand for 'Do Not Intubate'. It's the patient's order to her doctors and it draws an inviolable line. No breathing tubes, no ventilators, no call to the ICU for help.

I hurried back down the hall to the room. The sun had set, leaving the sky a dim purple. The room was dimmer still, the patient's face a sheen on the white pillow, her chest visibly stroking from the door. I stood in the doorway for a minute, watching her, trying not to match her breathing with my own. Her face was turned to me. The eyes glittered.

'How are you feeling?'

'Not. So. Hot.'

'I know,' I said. 'I'm going to get you some more oxygen.' I reached for the regulator in the wall and cranked it up to six litres, the maximum you can deliver by nasal cannula.

The nurse appeared at the door. 'Do you want me to call respiratory?'

'Yeah,' I said. 'That's good. Call respiratory.' Respiratory therapists know all sorts of tricks: complicated masks that somehow squeeze more oxygen into room-pressure air.

I went back to the workroom and paged Keith. It occurred to me that I was displaying weakness. I told myself I didn't care.

He called back in a minute, cheery, calm. 'What's up?'

I told him.

'She's DNR? You checked the chart?'

I set the phone down and found her chart. There in the 'Consents' section was the legal form, witnessed and signed.

'Yeah. DNR/DNI.'

'Well, that's it,' he said. 'If it's her time, it's her time. Just crank up her Os and give her some morphine. That's all you can do.'

There was silence for a minute.

'Do you need me to come up there?'

'No. I'm on it. It's okay. I'll call you if I need anything.'

'Okay. Have a good night.'

It was eight-thirty. I went back to the patient's room. A respiratory therapist had arrived, bearing a tangled mass of tubes and bags.

'What do you want her on?' The tech eyed the woman in the bed speculatively. 'Fifty per cent?'

'Let's try that.' I watched a minute as the tech unstrung his tubes, fitting valves together. The face on the pillow was blanker than ever now: she had closed her eyes. Without that glittering motion, her face looked as if it were simply waiting.

Half an hour later, the nurse found me again.
'Do you want me to do anything for twenty-six?'
'Like what?'
'She won't keep her mask on.'
'Why not?'
'She says she's claustrophobic.'
I threw my pen down on the desk.

The eyes were open again, looking out through the plastic skin. She was holding the face mask in her left hand, about a foot away from her face, as if restraining something that had tried to attack her. Her chest was still rising and falling too fast.

I went to the bedside and crouched beside her. The eyes slanted down with me, the head immobile on the bed. 'I won't,' she said, and pushed the mask into my hands.

'Why not?'
She shook her head. 'Can't.'
'Is it uncomfortable?'
'Suffocating. Can't.'
I bit back an argument. 'How about I give you something to help you relax?'
'Why?'
'You need the mask. You're not getting enough oxygen without it. If we can relax you a little, maybe you'll feel better about wearing it.'
The eyes closed for a moment. 'All right,' she said.
I told the nurse to give her a milligram of ativan and two of morphine, and to try to get the mask back on her.
Just after nine the nurse reappeared in the doorway of the workroom and shook her head.

'She won't keep the mask on.'

I pulled myself to my feet.

The patient was propped up in bed now, leaning forward, her hands braced on her thighs to support her. The posture is called 'tripoding'; it's something people do instinctively when they're having trouble getting air. Her shoulders were lifting and falling rhythmically with each breath. She was using what are called the accessory muscles, anything to help expand the ribcage with inhalation. It can buy you a little extra air exchange, but the price, in terms of exertion, is more than most of us can pay for very long. The mask lay in her right hand, hissing.

She didn't seem to notice me as I moved across the room; her gaze was straight ahead, intent on something. Each breath, I thought. Or perhaps something visible only to her through the far wall of the room.

'Mrs B?'

Her gaze flickered my way, a brief acknowledgement, then back to her inner vigil, intent.

My first impulse was to ask her how she was doing. I stifled it. I reached out instead and took the mask from her. Her hand was stiff; the fingers yielded slowly. Her eyes turned towards me.

'Does this bother you so much?' I held the mask out.

She nodded and drew away. As if it could bite her, I thought.

'More than the way you're feeling now?'

Her gaze clouded a moment. Unfair, I thought. Arguing with a dying woman.

She nodded again.

I sat at her bedside, holding the hissing plastic coil, looking into the mask. Reluctantly, unwilling to place my mouth where hers had been, I fitted the mask to my face, pressed the vinyl against my cheeks. I took a breath.

There was only a smell of plastic, then a high, eerily open sensation of emptiness. I took a breath, feeling my lungs expand; a vivid impression of spaces opening everywhere. I found her looking back at me, the eyes from the depths of her immobile face dark and liquid and alive.

I took the mask off. 'It makes you feel confined?'

She nodded, shrugged.

'Have you tried taking deep breaths?' I was still buzzing with the force of the oxygen; my lethargy and sleepiness were all gone. I felt ready to take this woman on and bring her with me to morning.

She looked at me only a moment before turning to the far wall again, shaking her head.

It occurred to me that she probably couldn't take deep breaths.

I was still holding the mask.

'Did the sedatives help any?'

No.

'Would you like to try some more?'

Shrug.

I went to find the nurse. We doubled the dose. I watched, this time, as the drugs ran in, saw the relaxation I hadn't believed the stiff skin could show, the subtle slumping of the shoulders. I waited and when sleep seemed about to take her I slipped the mask over her face. A hand stirred, rose a few inches, wavered, then fell to her lap; she settled back against the bed. I stood there beside her, holding the mask in place, watching. After a minute or two, we checked the pulse-ox: ninety-four per cent. Her respiratory rate was settling into the mid-twenties. Hours of accumulated tension dissipated from my own chest. The nurse and I walked quietly out the door. 'Keep an eye on her,' I said.

I don't remember what time the next call came. Probably around two. I was back in the workroom, running blearily over the results of the one o'clock draw, fielding pages from the floor. There had been a shift change at midnight, followed by a flurry of pages from the new shift coming on with questions. There was a patient down on 3 West who was refusing his prep for a scheduled colonoscopy.

I heard a knock and an unfamiliar face appeared in the doorway. 'Are you the doctor on call?' Shift change. I grunted something affirmative. 'Do you know the patient in twenty-six?'

An uncomfortable sensation stirred in my chest.

'I got report on her,' the new nurse said. 'Do you still want frequent vital signs?'

'How's she doing?'

'I don't know. Do you want me to check?'

'Please,' I said, and settled my head on my folded arms.

A hand shaking my shoulder. 'Doctor?'

I stirred unpleasantly. My face was stiff. My sleeve was wet.

'I'm sorry to bother you, but that lady in twenty-six, she's not looking so good.'

I sat upright.

'Her O_2 sat?' the nurse went on. 'It's only eighty-two. And her rate is over thirty.'

'Is she wearing her mask?'

'No.'

'Christ.' I was out of the room, stalking down the hall.

She lay in the bed, looking expectantly towards the door, the mask gripped in her hand. Her other hand went up as I approached, waving me away.

'Mrs B,' I called to her, pitching my voice as if into the distance.

The head bobbled for a moment, turned my way. The eyebrows were lifted slightly, but the skin above them was unfurrowed. The mouth was a hole air moved through.

'Mrs B,' I said again, willing her to look at me.

She did.

'You have to keep your mask on.' It did not sound so idiotic when I said it as it does now.

She shook her head.

'If you don't do it,' I said, reaching out to take the mask from her hand, 'you're going to die.' She made an ineffectual motion as I placed the mask over her face, looping the cord behind her head. Her hair was greasy with sweat. She reached up and placed a hand on the mask. My hand and her hand held it there. Did her breathing start to slow? I held the mask through one long minute, another. The nurse was a silhouette at the doorway. Another minute more, and I was sure the rate had fallen, the labouring of her shoulders lessened. To the nurse: 'Let's check a sat.'

Ninety-two per cent. To Mrs B, 'There. That feels better, doesn't it?' She nodded, faintly, and seemed to settle into the bed. I let my hand fall away from the mask, crooning, 'There, there.' After five minutes pressing the mask to her face, my outstretched arm felt like wood. I reached behind her head to snug the cord.

She pulled the mask away. 'I can't breathe. I don't want it,' she gasped. 'It's too tight.' And pulled harder until she snapped the cord in two.

I grabbed the mask and held it on her face. She reached up and clutched my wrist, and for a moment I thought we were about to struggle over it, but then she stopped and her hand fell away. Her eyes were fixed on mine.

The nurse was still at the doorway.

'Ativan,' I said. 'Two milligrams IV. And two of morphine.'

Mrs B still stared at me, her face remote and motiveless behind the mask. My arm was aching. Was I pressing the mask too hard? I eased up, fumbled with the broken cord, but the ends were too short to make a new one. Mrs B didn't take her eyes off mine as the nurse reached for the port in the IV tubing. Just as the nurse's fingers caught it she snatched her arm away.

'No.' The voice was a whisper.

'I can't then, Doctor,' the nurse said.

'What do you mean?'

'I can't force a patient. It would mean my licence.'

'She's going to die if she doesn't keep that mask on.'

'Then get psychiatry to declare her. But until then it's her decision. We can't make it for her.'

Psych wasn't going to declare her. I knew that. It was her decision. I knew that. But I couldn't let it end this way. Surely I could make her see.

'Mrs B,' I said finally, 'is there any way we can make this easier for you?'

'How about a bucket?' said the nurse.

My expression must have required explanation.

'A face tent, they call them. It's open at the top. It works for claustrophobia. Do you want me to call respiratory?'

'Please.'

The respiratory tech arrived after an interminable period during which Mrs B refused again and again to wear the mask. Eventually we found a compromise. She would hold it a few inches below her chin. It bumped the pulse-ox to eighty-eight per cent. But her respiratory rate continued to climb. I couldn't tell if it was anxiety or hypoxia. A blood gas would have told me, but I was reluctant to try. I didn't know what I would do with the information. When the tech arrived and fitted her with the bucket, I stood at the door watching. It seemed to be doing something.

The next page from twenty-six came around four. I had gone into the call room fifteen minutes before, but the moment I lay down it was clear there was no chance of sleep. I lay rigid in the lower bunk, unwilling even to turn out the light, bracing against the sensation of my pager at my hip. My thoughts were an incoherent jumble: scraps of medical education – the innervation of the hand, the watershed areas of the mesenteric circulation, drugs to avoid in supraventricular tachycardia – none of which was relevant to any of the calls I had gotten that night. I was thinking of anything but the patient in twenty-six, two floors overhead. The next page was, of course, about her.

The nurse picked up on the first ring. 'Doctor? I think you'd better get up here.'

I was out of the door without a word.

The scene in twenty-six was superficially unaltered. But from the bed I was hearing small whimpering noises, rhythmic, paced almost to the beating of my heart.

She was sitting bent over, the exaggerated movements of her chest and shoulders making her head rise and fall, rise and fall. I counted, but lost track in the twenties, somewhere around half a minute. At least forty.

'Mrs B?' I laid a hand on her shoulder. She didn't turn. Just the rapid rise and fall of the head. Her shoulder was clammy, her gown damp. Was she febrile? Was there something I'd missed? Should I have gotten cultures? Hung antibiotics? Was she having a PE? The body on the bed wasn't telling. Only the same carrier wave of distress, up and down, up and down. I looked to the door, where the nurse was standing. 'Get respiratory up here.' She started to go. 'And get me four of morphine.'

The patient didn't resist this time. I don't know if she was even aware, but as the plunger went down on the syringe I could see a change in her; she settled and her breathing slowed. The pulse-ox, which had been in the mid-seventies, climbed up a notch or two, settled in the low eighties. I had no idea if that was something she could live with. I stood at the bedside and watched. Her respiratory rate was in the low thirties. An eye opened, swivelled around the room until it met mine. The mouth moved, no sound came out.

'Mrs B,' I said, and my tone was frankly pleading now, 'you've got to let me help you.'

The eye held my gaze for a long moment, the dim gleam of the nightlight streaking across the cornea. A hand made a brief sweeping gesture, fell. Away.

Somewhere in the course of the night I had developed a fixed idea: if I could get her to morning, it would be okay. I had no idea where that notion came from. Years later, after what seems like countless midnight vigils, the trust and hope of it chill me. But then I clung like a child to the thought of morning. In the morning, her primary team would be on hand; someone would know what to do. By the light of the morning, ill spirits flee. In the morning, it would be off my hands.

The respiratory tech was at the door.

'It isn't working,' I said.

The tech didn't actually shrug. 'You don't think you can tube her?'

'I can't tube her,' I gritted out. 'DNI.'

'BiPAP?'

'I can't get her to wear an ordinary face mask.'

'Why don't you just snow her?'

It was a thought. She hadn't refused the morphine. I could try adding on sedation until she would let me put a mask on her – perhaps even a tight-fitting BiPAP mask, the next-best thing to intubation. It could be done.

'Yeah,' I said. 'Nurse? Bring me four of ativan. And another four of morphine.'

I had never given anyone so much sedation. I knew the risk: knock her out too far and her respiratory drive would suffer; she'd lose her airway; she'd suffocate.

But she was going to die this way, too. I watched, holding my breath as the drugs went in, trying to remember the doses of naloxone and flumazenil that would reverse these, if I had to.

Her breathing settled still more. Her eyelids fluttered and fell. 'Get a mask on her,' I said.

In a minute the tech had her fitted with an elaborate device that gripped her face like a diver's mask. There was no protest. The pulse-ox rose steadily to ninety, ninety-one, settled at ninety-two. I let out a sigh.

This time I did sleep. I must have, because my pager woke me from a dream of too many inscrutable objects, none of them fitting together, a puzzle I had to solve.

'Doctor? Twenty-six. She's fighting the mask.'

It was the same scene again. She was sitting up, crouched as if clutching some secret to her chest. The mask was pushed up on to her forehead. Her shoulders rose and fell, rose and fell. She didn't look up as I entered; her gaze lay burning on the opposite wall.

The pulse-ox was eighty-two.

I laid a hand on her shoulder, could feel her bones working as it rose and fell.

'Mrs B.'

She shook her head.
'We've got to do something.'
She shook it again.
'What can I do for you?'
Her hand waved me away.

I stood beside her, watching her breathe, for a very long time. She lay on the bed within reach of my outstretched hand, within the sound of my voice, but behind the wall of her fatigue and her breathlessness, sunk deep in her adamant gaze, she was unreachable. Unreachable by me. I wondered if she even knew I was still there, and felt suddenly a revulsion – not at her, but at my own presence in her room.

Her pulse-ox was eighty-two.

'Call me,' I said to the nurse, 'if she changes.'

Around six a.m. I was sitting in the call room, trying to shake myself awake. My pager went off. It was the eighth floor.

The room was different now. Light was striking in through the window, a dozen rising suns reflected off the opposite tower. The room was bright and still.

Fast asleep, even comatose, a living body moves. The chest expands, the nostrils flare, the eyelids twitch; pulses stir the skin, and over all of these there hovers an inarticulate hum of life. But a dead body is only that: dead, a body, given over to gravity and decay. The muscle tone that lends expression to the face is gone; the face is slack; the skin gone grey-green with the absence of blood (underneath, if you turn it over, you will find pooled at the backside a livid bruise).

I went through the motions of declaring death. Her eyes took my flashlight passively, the beam falling into the cloudy darkness of her pupils without a sign. I laid a stethoscope on her chest: only sporadic pings and creaks, sounds of a building settling in the night. Her flesh was cold, malleable, inert.

There were papers to fill out: organ donation, autopsy permission, the death certificate. I puzzled over 'Cause of death', wondering just what process I had failed to reverse.

'Respiratory failure,' I finally wrote, 'secondary to pulmonary fibrosis, secondary to systemic sclerosis.' The last line asked what underlying medical conditions (diabetes, hypertension, e.g.) contributed to the patient's demise. I looked at that a long time, and finally left it blank.

By the time I was done, the hospital had come to life around me. The intern who had signed out Mrs B to me scratched the name off her patient list.

Keith, the resident, appeared on the floor just before rounds got under way. 'How was your night?'

I told him. He listened to the story, pulled his lower lip, shook his head.

'You should have called me.'

I flinched. 'What would you have done?'

'Nothing,' he said. 'Just like you. There was nothing to do. But at least we could have done it together.' ■

WILLIAM T. VOLLMANN

Watching from the Mexican side, taken near Chula Vista, 1999

BODY SNATCHERS

William T. Vollmann

The All-American Canal was now dark black with phosphorescent streaks where the border's eyes stained it with yellow tears.

'These lights have been up for about two years,' Officer Dan Murray said. 'Before that, it was generators. Before that, it was pitch black.'

He was an older man, getting big in the waist, whose face had been hardened by knowledge into something legendary. For years he'd played his part in the work first begun by Eden's angel with the flaming sword, the methodical patrols and prowls to keep the have-not millions out of paradise – which in this case was Imperial County, California, whose fields of blondness, of endless pallid asparagus, onion plants like great lollipops and honey-coloured hay bales produced the lowest median tax income of any county in the state. Zone El Centro, named after the county seat, comprised Sectors 210 to 226, of which Sectors 217 to 223 happened to be Murray's responsibility. He kept the key to the armoury, whose rows of M4 shotguns awaited a mass assault from Southside which never came. He knew how to deploy the stinger

Border patrolmen guarding *pollos*, who pay to be taken across and travel together, in 1999. Many *solos*, who cross alone, are also caught

spikes, the rows of accordion-like grids like a row of caltrops: pull a string and they opened up to puncture a tyre. One car actually drove twelve desperate miles on four flat tyres until it was wrecked beyond any conceivable utility to its confiscators.

'They'll pop their heads up in a minute,' he was always saying. He was always right.

An hour ago we might have been able to see through the bamboo and across the wrinkled brown water into Southside where Mexicans sat on the levee waiting to seize their chance, but at that time Murray and I had been over by the Port of Entry east bridge where two Mexicans waited, not aliens yet; while on our side, Northside, another agent sat calmly watching them in his car.

'Hello,' said Murray. 'Have those folks been there all day?'

'Yessir,' the agent said.

Suddenly it was dusk, and the two men were already crossing. Now they were illegals.

'*Get out!*' an officer yelled at them. They turned and slowly, slowly walked back into Mexico across the humming throbbing bridge.

Then we drove west down the long horizon of border wall. Two Mexicans walked along the fence down in Southside, screaming obscenities at Murray.

'Now, you see, this has got concrete,' Murray explained. 'But it only goes down about four feet. They have their little spider holes. They pop up, throw a rock through the windshield, then go down again.'

We drove west, down into the lights of Calexico and out again, passing the sandy waste whose incarnation as a golf course was memorialized by carcasses of palm trees.

'See, another hole in the fence back there,' Murray said. 'Usually you just hold back and wait. They'll pop up.'

The golf course had gotten robbed once too often, and then somebody burned down the clubhouse after a fence-jumper from Southside was shot. So some townspeople told me. Their stories were weary and muddled, but in them as in this former golf course the border wall remained ever in the background, its long, rust-coloured fence dwindling into lights. Then the dim red fence abruptly ended, and we met the All-American Canal, which comprises so much of this sector's border westward of the wall. Follow the All-American upstream on a map, and you'll see that it abruptly turns north, wraps around Calexico International Airport near that abandoned golf course (the hollow in this spot is a good place for *pollos* and *solos* to hide, and sometimes for bandits, too, who murdered somebody here half a year ago), and then it bends due east again just before Comacho Road, ducking under the railway and Imperial Avenue, streaming on eastward towards its source, until the last we see of it, it's overlined the streets named after south-western riches: Turquoise Street, Sapphire Street, Garnet Street, Ruby Court, Emerald Way, Topaz Court – after which it runs off the map and out of Calexico. In the first four months of 1999 alone, eight people whom the authorities knew of had already drowned in the All-American's cool quick current, all of them presumably seekers of illegal self-improvement; and I imagine that other bodies were never found, being carried into jurisdictions where perhaps the non-human coyotes got them. In April 1999 the United

States Navy began to wire the canal with a 200,000-dollar noise-detection apparatus. *The goal is to create a system that can alert authorities when someone is in trouble in the canal*, my home newspaper informed me blandly. Who am I to doubt the navy's altruism?

'You should see these guys pickin' watermelon, bent over all day,' said Officer Murray. 'They do work most Americans wouldn't do.'

We were close by the Wistaria Check, which lay opposite the place on the Mexican side where the taxi driver and Juan the cokehead had taken me the day before.

The taxi driver had said, 'If you want, I'll jump into the canal and swim across, if you pay me.'

Juan, whose scrawny back and shoulders most proudly bore a tattoo of the Virgin for which he'd paid two US dollars back when he was twenty (he was now Christ's age), stopped the taxi to buy five hundred pesos' worth of powder in a twist of plastic. He was a true addict. Every day I had to advance him his wages. By late afternoon he needed a bonus. I had found him amidst the slow round of beggars and drunks on a street two blocks south of the United States where a poster announcing A MILLION DOLLAR FINANCIAL SERVICE depicted a giant identification card which among all its elysian proclamations faintly whispered NOT A GOVERNMENT DOCUMENT, then rushed on to proclaim ORDER YOUR PERSONAL US ID CARD HERE TODAY. On that hot afternoon when we departed Mexicali's red and yellow storefronts and drove westward into the dirt, the houses shrinking into shacks, Juan and the taxi driver kept glancing at me and muttering together; but I told them that I would have even more cash when I came back tomorrow. Far away, deeper into Mexico, I could see the pale bluish-white mountains like concretions of dust. Now we came into Juan's hometown where several of the Mexicali street whores lived, and although Juan wanted to stop to buy more coke, business, personified by me, demanded that we leave behind those long blocks of tiny houses of cracked dry mud whose yards were dirt instead of grass. So we turned on to a long dirt road in parallel to the All-American Canal, which we could not yet see. Here each of the many tiny cement or adobe houses was fenced away from the world. One fence derived from box spring bed frames. Other fence posts had been fashioned of twigs or columns of tyres, and there were many hedges of thorns on that nameless road of prickly pears, bamboo, dust, beautiful palm trees and turtles sleepily lurking in the stagnant ditchwater.

'See all those cars in there? *Stolen*,' my guide triumphantly explained. 'From America.'

'Well', I said, 'I'm glad they have a new home, Juan. How do you know they're stolen?'

'I don't think these people have enough money to buy a new car – or ten new cars.'

He said that in Mexicali it cost two or three hundred dollars for a brand-new stolen American automobile, which I considered not a bad price. He said that another industry of the householders along this road was to hide emigrants on consignment until nightfall, then help them try to swim the canal. And just as he finished explaining these matters, we came upon a man in sunglasses who was driving a brand-new van with tinted windows. We had seen no other vehicles before, and we saw none afterwards except for one water truck whose corroded white cylinder tank slowly bled water as it went. The man in sunglasses rolled down his night-dark window to study us, which was the only reason that we could see him at all. He was gripping a pair of binoculars against his face. When he had digested us, he drove slowly past, the window still down. He was watching the canal now through his binoculars.

'Think he's a coyote?' I asked.

'What else?'

Now we arrived at a little shrine to the Virgin and a cross. Someone had died, perhaps a *solo*. Juan read the inscription. Yes, he said, the man had drowned trying to cross into America, where everything was wider, cleaner, safer, more expensive, more controlled and more homogeneous. And by this shrine we parked the car and ascended the levee of crumbing mud dust to gaze at the United States, where of the three of us only I could legally go. It was hot and thorny and dry on

Searching for illegals on the 'Ho Chi Minh Trail', east of Calexico, 1999

the Mexican side with all those American fields appearing so cruelly green like paradise, *because the water belongs to America*, as Juan put it. Beside us, a skinny horse browsed in garbage.

Some chocolate-brown boys were swimming in the coffee-coloured canal, and on Northside, very close to Wistaria Check as I said, a white truck was parked and two middle-aged white men were trying their luck at catfishing, ignoring the boys who ignored them. Juan pointed to the boys and said, 'See those poor people over there? They're gonna try for the night-time, then they'll walk through all the fields...'

'Ask them where they're going.'

They're gonna go to Canada, they say, unless Border Patrol catch them.

'Ask them if they know where Canada is.'

They say they don't know, but somebody told them it's a real nice country where you don't get hassled like you do in America.

On our side, the dusty desert side, an obelisk marked American dominion, and later I learned from the Border Patrol that the canal actually lay slightly north of the true border, but those guardians found it needlessly troublesome to assert their authority over the few slender feet of United States sovereignty between the marker and the water. Officer Murray said to me, 'If I saw people on the Southside of the canal, I'd just wave to 'em. You see a raft, now, you just back off. Don't wanna spook anybody.'

A day or two later the local papers carried a story about how Border Patrol agents had shot one of those rafts with a pellet gun. The raft capsized, and one or two aliens drowned. (There are Border Patrol officers in boats, and they're like *fishing*, a *solo* in Algodones told me. They cut open or shoot at the rafts and let 'em drift downriver. 'Last night there were about seven shots,' his comrade said, shrugging.) But the drownings, I hope, were an aberration. I never at any time met a *solo* or *pollo* who expressed physical fear of the Border Patrol. Murray insisted that some agents bought fast food with their own money for the frightened Southside kids they'd captured.

'But the Mexican consulate never hears that,' Murray said bitterly. 'They'll probably start rafting pretty soon.'

He stood listening to the canal, which was long, low, black with bamboo. His job was not to shape the destiny of those who sought America, but merely to postpone it. For what could he do to them but lock them in a holding cell, then deport them back to Southside so that they could try again? And for a moment, as we stood there, each of us letting his private thoughts fall into the pit of the night, I almost pitied the futility of his occupation, as I suspect he did mine, but then I fortunately persuaded myself that all vocations and callings are equally futile. He talked about how beautiful it was when he patrolled the shoulder of an onion field at dusk with the bees returning to their hives, and I started to like him. He told me about the fine catfishing he'd had in the canal, and we gazed at the sparse weak lights which shone from Mexico, until suddenly the radio said, 'There's already a rope across. Looks like it'll be near Martin Ranch.'

'Okay,' said Murray, 'I'm up on the canal bank.'

'Okay, copy,' replied the radio.

'They could be running across the fields right now,' he said to me.

'Okay, he's got sign.'

We were in the car now, speeding towards the place. We stopped by a wall of hay, which we smelled more than saw in the dark humid night. Border Patrolmen were searching with their lights.

'Right here you got the traffic,' Murray said, and he shone his flashlight on fresh footprints in the sand. 'These kids should be easy to catch,' he went on, half talking to himself. 'But I feel naked; I don't have a spotlight. I don't have any alleylights...'

The long field appeared green through an agent's nightscope. The Border Patrolmen hunted and searched, as the crumbly earth devoured their feet up to the ankles. It was silt from the days of the ancient sea. They came through the field, stalking it with headlights which rendered the furrows cruelly bright.

'Maybe we'll find the bodies,' Murray said. 'Maybe not. It's just pure luck. But these kids tripped a sensor.'

'I can't see 'em any more,' another officer said, resting his hands on his Sam Browne belt.

'I got an eye on your bodies,' said the nightscope man, whose monitor made the word *bodies* seem chillingly appropriate, for in the green night the aliens glowed white like evil extraterrestrial beings or zombies out of a science fiction movie. The nightscope man could also reverse the contrast if he chose, so that the *bodies* became green silhouettes in a glowing white field of nightness.

'They're layin' up in the middle of the field,' he went on, directing the hunters through a darkness which neither they nor the aliens, who surely thought themselves safe, could penetrate. How eerie it was! Only the nightscope man could see! The aliens lurked on faith that the darkness was their invincible friend. The Border Patrolmen could scarcely perceive where they set their own feet; they could have been approaching a precipice; but they drew near the unseen *bodies* with equal and, as it proved, more justified faith.

'Lookin' dead smack in the middle,' said the nightscope man. 'Yeah, I got a fix on your bodies. Turn left. Three steps more. Another coupla steps. They should be right in front of you, right down there in those... Yeah, you got 'em.'

Now came the wide circle of the spotlight. The hunters' cars circled the field. And the *bodies*, hopelessly silhouetted, resurrected themselves from the fresh earth, giving in to capture and deportation. They rose, becoming black on black. And the shadow of a man whose hands were on his head was replicated manifold. Two of them with their hands on their heads stood gazing down at the half-empty jugs of water they'd carried. Sad and submissive faces gazed into the darkness, half-blinded by the brightness as the Border Patrolmen frisked them. Yes, the *bodies* stood wide-eyed in the light, all in the line, with their hands obediently behind them. Coughing, shuffling, they began to cross the fields.

'You know what?' a Border Patrolman said to one of the *bodies*. 'You really need to brush your teeth. You've got wicked bad breath, guy.'

The *body* was silent. In the nightscope it had been as white as one of the freshly dead fish in the cool green poison (or should I say 'reputed poison'?) of the Salton Sea. Now it began to reveal itself to be brown – Hispanic, sunburnt and field-stained.

'Let's go, *amigos*. Come on. Let's go; let's go.'

None of the captives looked terrified. It was as Officer Murray had said: People realize they're not going to jail for the rest of their lives, so they calm down.

'Now, that irrigator's car over there just happens to be in a convenient place,' an agent was saying. 'We'll have to check him out…'

The Mexicans walked more quickly now, carefully cradling their water jugs, attended by the bright, bright lights. Now they sat in a line on the roadside, a long line of them, with their jugs and bottles of water between their legs. Most of them wore baseball caps. They were young, wiry, strong to work. Their eyes shone alertly in the night. Already resigned, they quickly became philosophical, and in some cases even cheerful, slapping their knees and poking one another smilingly in the ribs. Soon they'd join the people staring out the panes of the holding cells. After eight hours or so, if they had no criminal history, they'd be sent back to Mexico.

'We got some that made the river, but we bagged the rest of 'em,' an officer was saying, but already the Border Patrol had found other game.

'Two made it up into the housing development,' a woman's excited voice cried on the radio, 'but we're tryin' to inch up on 'em…'

THE GARDENS OF PARADISE

What did the *bodies* come here for? We all know the answer. I remember how on one of my many bus rides south I was meditating on the heat and strangeness of this corner of California when the man beside me awoke, and turned towards the window like a plant towards the sun. Soon we would come to the sign which read IMPERIAL COUNTY LINE and a few minutes later we'd pass the Corvina cafe, which would surely be as closed and dead as one of those corvina floating belly-up in the Salton Sea.

The man sat gazing alertly eastward across the desert flats towards the long deep green stripe of date plantations and the dusty red and blue mountains beyond. I inferred that this landscape was his by birth or long residence. Perhaps he had been away from it for a while. He'd told me that he was coming from a Fourth of July party at his sister's, but I'd seen the policeman standing in the loading area, watching to make sure that he boarded this bus whose disinfectant, pretending to be pine or lemon, stung the nose with its bad chemical smell. He'd slept with his chin in his hands all the way from Indio and past the tan silence of the Jewel Date Company's former factory parallel to the railroad tracks where rusty flatbed cars gave off heat. Now he sighed a little, and turned towards me as eagerly as he had strained towards the mountains. He offered me Mexican candy, praising it because it was cheap. Open-handed, gruff and husky, he longed to tell the tale of his life. He'd served twenty-four years in the Spanish army – or maybe he'd been an American soldier stationed in Spain, this fine point being occluded by his broken English and my ignorance of Spanish. At any rate, Spain had failed him, evidently by means of woman trouble. Now he was living in El Centro to be near his eighty-two-year-old father who had once been a mechanical genius but who lately did little more than putter around the air conditioner, trying to grow coolness like a vegetable and then inbreed and harvest it. When he spoke of his father, tenderness came into his voice in just the same way that the yellow flowers of the palo verde tree come briefly back even in July or August if there is rain. His father was too old to drive a car, so once our bus pulled into the El Centro station, my friend would be walking home in the 110-degree heat, which killed illegal aliens easily.

The ones who crossed alone were called *solos*. The ones who paid to be taken across were *pollos* – chickens. And who better to shepherd chickens through dangerous ways than a *coyote*? That's truly what they were called! Coyotes never eat chickens, do they? (Every day, many *pollos* die, a taxi driver told me with solemn exaggeration. The newspaper said that only 254 illegals had died last year, to which the taxi driver replied. 'Liars – assassins! Two or three a day die right here!

An onion field in full flower, east of Calexico

They hide the bodies under the sand so that the Border Patrol won't see.' 'They do die,' a lifetime *pollo* later told me, but not that many.) Then there were the chicken-handlers, the *pollistas* or *polleros* whom the big-shot coyotes deputed to do the dirty work of canal crossings and the like. Officer Murray called them 'scouts'. 'They're pretty chicken,' he said, not meaning the pun.

Like their bosses, they sometimes ran away when it was dangerous, leaving their passengers to die of thirst. For it was so very hot! When his father died, my seat-mate might move away from Imperial County, on account of the heat. In his low, hoarse, not unpleasant voice, he remarked that he didn't mind sitting outside in 105 degrees, but when it got up to 115 then his cold beer turned into hot coffee, and it was time to go indoors. He uttered many a melancholy jest of this character. I'd already begun to think of him as *the old soldier*, and was almost appalled that he was my age, thirty-eight; he looked twenty years older. This working man, dark and wiry, had resisted many solar assaults, armoured by no more than an upturned cap-brim, but each attack had shrivelled him a little more, so that he'd eventually be desiccated to his very soul. The hot, dry sunlight instantly warms flesh to a state near burning, then cauterizes it and stains it brown. Born in Brawley, which our Greyhound soon would reach, he'd never been to the Salton Sea in his entire life. (How far was it? Half an hour's drive?) As a boy he'd been too busy in the fields, he said; after that he'd tried his luck in Spain. And now as we continued south on Highway 111 he began to explicate the crops to me, each time weighing himself down with a new story of dreary and dangerous drudgery.

Here came another date orchard to our left, with busy birds silhouetted in the palm crests, uplifting their beaks, clicking and crying even in the heat of midday. I admired the shade and luxurious fruit of those trees, but the old soldier turned to me with a bitter smile and said that the most perilous labour of his life had been ascending towards the birds on a rickety ladder leaned against each tree in turn, with no one holding the bottom for him; his job was to tie bags around immature dates so that they'd not be lost. Little and lean, he'd scampered into the sun which burned him until he resembled the black fly with alert yellow eyes which one often finds crouching in the dusty crease of a palm's fan. Sometimes he got dizzy; sometimes the ladder slipped. His memories were stained with terror.

By the time he'd finished speaking, our Greyhound bus had drawn close to an onion field in glorious flower, and the old soldier croaked out that working in the onion fields had left him stinking of onion juice, his eyes watering day and night. After a week the onion juice was literally under his skin. (I thought of what Officer Murray had said: 'When you get people out of an onion field, you wanna roll your windows down.') No matter how long he bowed beneath the showerhead, scrubbing himself red, the onion smell kept oozing out of him so that he stank even to himself and coughed himself to sleep. Eventually he began to bring up blood from too much coughing.

'No, I hung it up,' the old soldier said. 'Don't wanna pick in the fields no more. I got me a ladyfriend, she about forty, forty-five years

old. And every morning she drives from El Centro all the way to Yuma.
There are four of them people; they share gas. Then she picks. Imagine
that, a forty-five-year-old lady and still out there picking! What a tough
gal! One time she brought me a cantaloupe from the field. Another
time, it was a big watermelon...'

And he smiled a smile of loving pride. But then his bitterness
landed on him again, like flies on a sweaty face. We'd come to a place
of white puffballs left behind in the dark fields. The old soldier said that
they were cantaloupes – no plants, only the pale spheres sticking out.
The migrant workers would turn them up later. He had been among
the up-turners of cantaloupes and of so many other crops, following
the harvesters on foot, gleaning up lost fruits under that hot, dusty,
greyish-white sky. He began to tell me how it was, waving his withered
hands as he angrily, dolefully whispered, describing the ache between
the shoulder blades, the throbbing in the small of the back, the shooting
pains in the arms, the hands that after gripping and lifting all day
became dirt-stained baseball mitts which could no longer open or
close, painfully throbbing in the bones. Beyond these agonies he
remembered with all his hatred the Imperial summers, which had
moved one woman on a hundred-degree Saturday evening in Indio to
tell me how she had realized that this planet truly orbits a star of
immense heat and brightness; whenever she stepped outside on an
Imperial day, she could keep possession of only a slender slice of
moments before being overpowered by stuporous confusion. Once she
was safely back inside, everything on her person, every key or card,
every square inch of her blouse, gave off heat. And yet the migrant
workers had to spend all day outside, sometimes working for less than
the legal minimum wage. The old soldier had finished with that. He
could not bear it any more.

The *Imperial Valley Press* stood on his side. In a section entitled OUR
OPINION: TIME FOR A CHANGE, that newspaper laid out the problem:

> As important as agriculture is to the county, there are limits on a
> community with an economy so dependent on farming, because

agricultural workers do not exactly get the highest salaries... Finally, agriculture is not as strong in the Imperial Valley as it has been in years past.

The *Press* slavered over the smoothly named *Gateway to the Americas Project*, which would soon erect houses and industrial parks near the new Calexico East Port of Entry. It could create thousands of jobs. The hoped-for future of the Imperial Valley: strip malls, office parks, chain stores, Los Angelesization. Meanwhile the old soldier's ladyfriend went on fruit-picking, and in hopes of doing the same thing the *pollos* and *solos* slithered up and down the border fence. ∎

CONTRIBUTORS

Deborah Boliver Boehm is a translator, editor and travel writer. Her books include *A Zen Romance*, *Ghost of a Smile*, and translations of *The Tattoo Murder Case* and *The Cat in the Coffin*. She lives in Santa Fe.

Catherine Cobham teaches Arabic language and literature at the University of St Andrews and has translated a number of Arab writers, including Naguib Mahfouz, Yusuf Idris, Hanan al-Shaykh and Fuad al-Takarli.

Margaret Jull Costa has translated many Portuguese, Spanish and Latin American writers, among them Javier Marías, Bernardo Atxaga, Fernando Pessoa and José Saramago.

Mahmoud Darwish (1941–2008) was born in Upper Galilee, Palestine. He fled with his family to Lebanon in 1948 and after returning to the newly formed state of Israel, he began writing poetry. In 1988, he wrote the Palestinian Declaration of Independence. *A River Dies of Thirst: A Journal* will be published in September.

Rana Dasgupta's first novel, *Tokyo*

Cancelled, was shortlisted for the 2005 John Llewellyn Rhys Prize. His second, *Solo*, was published earlier this year. He lives in Delhi.

Tamas Dobozy is the author of two collections of stories, *When X Equals Marylou* and *Last Notes*. He lives with his family in Kitchener, Ontario and teaches twentieth-century American literature at Wilfrid Laurier University.

Mitch Epstein's photographs are held in major museum collections, including the Metropolitan Museum of Art, New York, and the J. Paul Getty Museum, Los Angeles. The photographs in this issue are taken from *American Power*, published in September.

Mary Gaitskill is the author of *Bad Behaviour*, *Two Girls, Fat and Thin*, *Because They Wanted To* and, most recently, *Veronica*, a novel, and *Don't Cry*, a collection of stories.

Terrence Holt practises and is on the faculty at the University of North Carolina School of Medicine. He is the author of a forthcoming collection of short stories, *In the Valley of the Kings*.

FIGHTING AIDS ONE BOOK AT A TIME

"One of the hottest literary hubs in New York: the bookstore salon that the city has been missing." *– The New York Times*

126 Crosby St.
(between Houston and Prince Streets)
New York, New York 10012
(212) 334-3324
www.housingworks.org/bookstore
Monday-Friday, 10-9; Saturday, 12-7, Sunday, 12-7

Jackie Kay's memoir *Red Dust Road* will be published by Picador next year. Her short stories, *Wish I was Here*, won the Decibel Prize and she last appeared in *Granta* 98 with the story 'The Last of the Smokers'.

Javier Marías's novels include the trilogy *Your Face Tomorrow*, the third volume of which, *Poison, Shadow and Farewell*, will be published in November. His work has been translated into thirty-seven languages. 'Bad Nature' was published in *Granta* 66.

Kenzaburō Ōe's books include *A Personal Matter, Teach Us to Outgrow Our Madness, Hiroshima Notes, A Quiet Life*, and *Rouse Up O Young Men of the New Age!* He won the Nobel Prize for literature in 1994.

Will Self's latest book is *Liver*. He first appeared in *Granta* 43 in 1993 when he was named a Best of Young British Novelist, and last appeared in *Granta* 104 with 'The Fount of All Smoky Wisdom'.

Lionel Shriver is the author of nine novels, including *The Post-Birthday World* and *We Need to Talk About Kevin*. Her new novel, *Time is*

Money, will be published in spring 2010. She is a frequent contributor to the *Sunday Times*, the *Guardian*, *The Economist*, the *Daily Telegraph* and the *New York Times*.

Rupert Thomson's novels include *The Insult, The Book of Revelation* and *Death of a Murderer*. 'Call Me By My Proper Name' is taken from his forthcoming memoir, *This Party's Got To Stop*.

William T. Vollmann is the author of nine novels, including *Europe Central*, which won the National Book Award. He has also written three collections of stories, a memoir, and four works of non-fiction.

Sam Willetts was born in 1962. He has worked as a teacher, journalist and travel writer. His first poetry collection, *New Light for the Old Dark*, will be published early next year.

Contributing Editors
Diana Athill, Jonathan Derbyshire, Sophie Harrison, Isabel Hilton, Blake Morrison, Philip Oltermann, John Ryle, Sukhdev Sandhu, Lucretia Stewart.